ASIA

NORTH
AMERICA

FAR
EAST

JAPAN

HAWAII

W9-BEX-360

Pacific Ocean

Ocean

AUSTRALIA

NEW ZEALAND

Ray Manley's WORLD IN FOCUS

Iguassu Falls, *Brazil-Argentina*

Ray Manley's WORLD IN FOCUS

Photography by Ray Manley

Text by Eleanor Elliott Ullmann

Introduction by Barry Goldwater

MKPpress

TUCSON, ARIZONA

All photographs from the files of Shostal Agency, New York City

Edited by Kit Scheifele
Designed by Stanley G. Fabe
Typography by Tucson Typographic Service, Inc.
Color Separations by Alfred S. Johnson
Lithographed by Shandling Lithographing Co., Inc., Tucson
Bound by Roswell Bookbinders, Phoenix, Arizona

Photograph of Bay Bridge by Mickey Prim, M. Photog.
Photograph of Tower Bridge by Naurice Koonce, M. Photog.

All photographs made with 5x7 Linhof, 121 mm (wide angle), 180, 210 mm (normal), 340 mm (long) Schneider lenses on 5x7 Ektachrome.

Copyright © 1968, by M K P Press
All Rights Reserved / Printed in the U.S.A.
Library of Congress Catalog Card Number: 68-19143

About the Photographer . . .

RAY MANLEY'S WORLD IN FO-CUS was conceived some years ago when Ray realized that such often-photographed places as the Eiffel Tower or the Taj Mahal could still be photographed differently and dra-matically — thus conveying to the reader a different feeling. This dis-covery took him on three around-the-world trips of four months each, a five-month European trip, plus two long journeys to South America and the South Pacific.

A native of Cottonwood, Arizona, Manley first gained national recognition in *Arizona Highways* magazine. In 1954 he formed Ray Manley Commercial Photography in Tucson. This firm, now greatly expanded, has industrial assignments nearly everywhere in the world. In 1960 Manley earned the coveted pro-fessional title of Master Photographer.

With his wife and devoted companion, Ruth, he has traveled at least 40,000 miles each year since 1947. His photographs are in constant use by airlines, in travel brochures, on record-album covers, in other ad media, textbooks, and *Arizona Highways,* to which he is still a regular contributor.

About the Author . . .

— Lynn Sanders, M. Photog.

FEW PEOPLE have traveled more intelligently, nor with more verve and awareness, than ELEANOR ELLIOTT ULLMANN. Her training for observation began at an early age, for she was blessed with a mother who had a profound love of nature which she imparted to the young Eleanor while also teaching her to observe carefully. In high school an interest in writing was fostered by wise teachers, and this has stood Mrs. Ullmann in good stead throughout her life and implemented her talent for "seeing."

She was fortunate in her marriage to Herbert Ullmann, who inspired her love of travel, for he was happily willing to share what became his wife's vital interests, and managed to combine a successful career in business with an avocation which eventually made virtual professionals of them both. Their travels began early and have continued throughout their lives, taking them to every corner of the world, beginning with a thorough grounding in and knowledge of their own vast and wonderful United States.

Their trips have been planned with the utmost care and study that they might profit from all they saw. From the beginning Mrs. Ullmann went armed with notebooks and typewriter, and her carefully and excitingly written journals served as letters home when their children were not with them.

The outgrowth of what began as a hobby of great seriousness for both of them finally put them in the professional bracket. Portions of Mrs. Ullmann's journals were expanded into articles on nature and travel for various magazines and the couple has lectured as a team on significant platforms across the country.

For their outstanding contributions, both Mrs. Ullmann and her husband have been honored by being named Fellows of the American Geographical Society.

Monument Valley, *Arizona-Utah*

DURING the twelve years that I served in the United States Senate I was assured each day of a cheery and bright beginning because, as I walked into my office, I saw on the walls of the reception room six very large photographic murals of my native Arizona done by that fine artist and my good friend, Ray Manley. For years Ray has been giving Arizonans and all Americans — in fact, people all over the world who read *Arizona Highways* magazine — an intimate, colorful, and exact insight into the beauties of my state. He is a photographer who has mastered the tools of his trade and uses them well. He presents to the viewer a picture, artfully and beautifully composed, faithfully reproduced, and with total qualities — whether the picture is in black and white or in color — that give one the feeling that he is looking at the actual subject and not the reproduction.

When Ray told me of his plans to produce a book which would step outside of Arizona and include pictures he has taken on his many travels around the world I was delighted — not only because I knew it would be a magnificent book but, even more importantly, because I knew that through the lens of his camera Ray would bring a wider knowledge to the reader of what one can see around the world.

The more I have traveled across the length and breadth of America and around the globe visiting different countries, the more I have become convinced that as people begin to know each other better, to understand each other's problems and to be able to visualize how each of our many nations live, the closer we will come to achieving world peace. Yet travel is not essential to such understanding, because the ever-increasing use of good photography makes possible a knowledge of other countries and peoples without leaving home. *Arizona Highways* magazine, for example, has become a world-known institution and people in Stockholm or Bangkok or the Philippine Islands can talk knowledgeably about Arizona because of the excellence of the photographs and articles appearing in that magazine.

I have found some beautifully done magazines and books of photography on parts of Africa, Australia, France, the Scandinavian countries, the Asiatic countries and others, and when I have visited these places it seems that I have been there before, so clearly has the impression of the different scenes remained in my mind. I feel I know the people better, too, because having had a chance to see pictures of them and their country it's pretty much like walking into a town in America that one hasn't visited in some time and feeling as though one is able to say hello to the townspeople, and certainly the architecture, the streets, and the scenery ring a familiar bell.

Photography is certainly not the total answer to this need of better and wider knowledge and understanding, but it plays an important role toward this end. This book will, I feel sure, make the reader feel that travel is possible even without leaving the comfort of his armchair.

But this is much more than a picture book. Accompanying each photograph is a stimulating, informative, concise text. Eleanor Elliott Ullmann, who has also written for *Arizona Highways* and other magazines, has given a host of facts unknown to most of us which greatly enhance the appreciation of the photographs. Her wide travels and painstaking research are evident in the text of Ray's book.

As you read through this book, as you look at the pictures, keep in mind that they were taken by a man who many years ago decided that photography would be his life's work and who, in the intervening years, has so mastered this art that he is today recognized as one of the fine photographers of the world. This volume also serves to remind us that no matter how high one sets his sights, if an individual really wants, really works, and really drives, he will reach his goal. Ray has reached his in this volume.

Ray has given us a valuable and different contribution — a book for the library of every person who seeks authenticity combined with beauty. It will certainly serve as a challenge to other photographers everywhere. I am honored to have been asked to write the introduction to it.

To a fellow photographer and a fellow Arizonan, thanks, Ray, for a wonderful job.

BARRY GOLDWATER

Phoenix, Arizona

A Personal Note

This book really got its start in 1958 when a fast-talking promoter invited me to join him in a plan to photograph seventeen European countries — their symbolic places of interest, landmarks and native costumes. These pictures were to be used in promoting tourism for a European airline. Never having been to Europe, I spent five months researching picture possibilities in these countries. I soon found that while places of renown were beautifully described in the travel media, no one had taken the trouble to give any information concerning the relative orientations of the camera subjects — that is, the way the Leaning Tower of Pisa leaned, or in which direction the Little Mermaid in Copenhagen faced. Perhaps this makes little difference to some people, yet all these places would be more memorable and interesting — especially to photographers — if they could be seen or photographed at the right time of day when the sunlight was at a good angle.

A few days before our planned departure to Europe — after vaccinations, passports and hotel reservations had been secured and plane tickets purchased — I found that the promoter had caught a plane out of Los Angeles, leaving no forwarding address at his hotel. By this time *bon voyage* parties had been given for my wife, Ruth, and me, articles had appeared in local papers about our trip and we decided just to proceed as planned and make the same sort of pictures anyway. We had arranged a busy itinerary and in four month's time we traveled through most of Europe. Fortunately, we arrived at about half of our destinations at the right time of day. But I kept wondering how much more efficient any trip could be if one knew in advance the right time of year and day that any given attraction was best photographed. Tours are, for the most part, well planned in this regard, but even these could be improved and many people travel independently or have free time during tours for observing and photographing.

Bolstered by the financial success of our trip, Ruth and I continued our travels to the world's major attractions, alternating between our own beautiful United States, Canada and Mexico

with trips to the South Pacific, Europe and three lengthy trips zigzagging around the world. New locations always brought the same old problem — which way does Angkor Wat face and is the Taj Mahal an afternoon or morning picture? Because we did not have the answers, we added extra days to the itinerary to allow sufficient time for good weather and the right time of day. Often when we did arrive at the right time, we then had several days of waiting after completing the photography due to infrequent flights or other transportation problems which might have been avoided with better advance knowledge.

The more we traveled and the more pictures I made, the more eager I became to publish a book of photogenic places around the world that would include just the kind of information we had necessarily to find out for ourselves. Finally, in the winter of 1966 the decision was made to publish a book of some one hundred of the world's most photogenic places that one could visit on an extended trip around the world, including a few locations off the usual paths. Nearly all those included here can be reached easily by normal transportation. One includes a short horseback ride, one is reached by helicopter, and one by small aircraft. For each picture we have included the relative focal length of the lens for any camera, the time of day each photograph was made and the direction the camera faced. Additional information concerning exposure or unusual problems that might arise is also included.

In many instances the photograph published was made with the most desirable light. This necessitated, in numerous cases, long waits or returning for better weather years later. However, I would be the first to admit that others were made with only the best light available at the time. Often the weather just wasn't good. If a few of your favorite subjects are missing, it may be that the weather was so poor that I refused to photograph a magnificent monument or mountain with the light available. Fuji in Japan is a subject that has eluded my camera on three occasions for periods of up to three weeks each. The rose-colored city of

Petra is missing due to the six-day Arab-Israeli War. I was only a few miles from Petra two days before the hostilities began but it seemed unwise at the time to risk all the accumulated exposed film I was carrying going through Jordanian customs. In Russia, St. Basil's Cathedral was covered with scaffolding as were all the public buildings in Leningrad in preparation for Russia's fiftieth anniversary celebration of the Revolution.

Recently, on my third attempt to photograph Iguassu Falls, Brazil, luck was with me. The Iguassu River meanders from its source in Brazil through miles of green jungle until it reaches the edge of a gorge 285 feet beneath it. Here the tempo changes as the river drops from the brow of the elongated horseshoe-shaped shoreline into the gorge below. Iguassu is a multiple falls separated by small islands of tropical vegetation. Some of the falls are interrupted in their descent and form shimmering pools. Sixteen miles below the falls the Iguassu River joins the great Paraná. Every man has his own superlatives but to me the grandeur and aesthetic beauty of Iguassu Falls rates foremost. This is the answer to a photographer's search for incomparable perfection in nature.

Probably the most important decision that had to be made after the book began to take shape in my mind was the selection of the person to write the text. From the outset the volume was obviously a photo book, but mere captions could not give it meaning and worth. To make the book valuable to travelers as well as to others, it must have accurate, interesting and helpful information. Yet I didn't wish to produce another geography book or an "all beautiful" travel come-on. Someone suggested that I find a "name" writer. But I felt it important that the writer be a seasoned traveler who had visited most of the places pictured and who could give an honest, informative word picture that would complement each color reproduction. Such a person is Eleanor Elliott Ullmann, a world traveler with her husband for many years and a woman with a lively curiosity about and interest in our world. Mrs. Ullmann and her photographer husband, Herbert, traveled with Ruth and me in some sections of our last around-the-world trip. Her inquisitive nature, her desire to get the last bit of information that would enhance the value of the book, convinced me that I was extremely fortunate when Mrs. Ullmann consented to do the writing. I give my heartfelt thanks to her for the many months she devoted to the research and writing.

The final selection of photographs from the thousands that were considered did result in some compromise from my own personal choices, for I am partial to the natural wonders of the world. However, to give well-rounded coverage of the world's most famous places, it is necessary to include photographs of much of man's architecture. I hope the variety that is included here pleases the serious traveler who knows many of these places where millions of people travel year after year.

Two of the pictures included were taken by my partners and good friends whom I especially wish to thank for their continued help and encouragement. The San Francisco Bay Bridge was photographed by Mickey Prim, while the Tower Bridge, London, is by Naurice Koonce.

And that's the background of WORLD IN FOCUS. It's ironical that this volume and my many travels outside of North America began with a hoax, and that to "save face" I went ahead with no assurance that anything would come of that trip. Secretly, I was thankful that I had been a gullible westerner who thought a man's word was his bond and had believed this man whose idea was sounder than his character.

I might have attempted such a trip later anyway, but at that point in my life, to invest four months' time and more money than I'd ever spent on anything took a lot of self-convincing. Should that promoter read this book, I halfway dedicate it to him, though it is formally dedicated to my travel companion and helper, my wife Ruth.

RAY MANLEY

Tucson, Arizona

World in Focus / CONTENTS

Bay Bridge / San Francisco, California

THE ERA OF SOCIABLE FERRY BOATS, OFTEN DUBBED "FLOATing clubhouses," ceased when the San Francisco-Oakland Bay Bridge was opened in 1936. This enormous vehicular artery eight and a quarter miles long with its two decks accommodating high-speed traffic, supplanted the 20-to-45-minute interlude in the life of the businessman crossing the bay morning and evening. At Yerba Buena Island the traffic bullets through a well-lighted tunnel. The entire bridge is illuminated with yellow sodium-vapor lights which pierce fog. But the man at the wheel sees only the white road lines and competing traffic. No longer does he enjoy the magnificent expanse of blue water nor dwell upon the early tales of San Francisco Bay.

In 1579 the English sea raider Sir Francis Drake, in his *Golden Hinde,* sailed right past the mile-wide entrance to this bay and never saw it. In 1595 the Spaniard Cermano in his galleon did likewise. Both anchored and enjoyed the hospitality of the primitive California Indians in what is today known as Drake's Bay, under Point Reyes. There are credible stories that both explorers named that bay San Francisco. In 1775 yet another Spaniard, Juan Manuel de Ayala, put his small ship through the treacherous waters of the Golden Gate to enter the great bay which he promptly named San Francisco. The name has remained.

None of these four men did much more than look and leave, but in 1776 Juan Bautista de Anza and his lieutenant Moraga rooted the first Spanish colony, Yerba Buena (referring to a mint herb found here), in a cove of the bay where the city of San Francisco arose later.

Ambitious English and Russians entertained the possibility of possessing this bay area, but Charles Frémont, United States explorer and political leader, in 1846 barged over the mountains and planted the American flag on the bay's shore. Mexico and the United States were at war and American warships sailed into the bay to support his claim. California was ceded by Mexico to the United States and the unfragrant Yerba Buena Cove became San Francisco. Frémont named the harbor's entrance the Golden Gate, but his supposition that it resembled Constantinople's Golden Horn was slightly awry. Then in 1849 the mad gold rush of the Forty-Niners was in full swing. Men took their pay in bits of gold wire, either short or long. Two short bits equalled a U.S. twenty-five-cent piece, and from this usage "two-bits" has become a dictionary-accepted word.

In 1931 the old name of Yerba Buena was attached to Goat Island in the middle of the bay and the name acquired more "fragrance." Another Spanish name which stuck is Alcatraz — named from the flock of pelicans on this island.

San Francisco Bay is a sprawling nucleus of big cities, industries, business, shipping, fishing and suburban life. It harbors merchant, Navy, passenger ships and private craft. The great vertical movement of the bay tides, twice daily, plus the strong and changing currents caused by the Sacramento and San Joaquin rivers make navigation here a precise art. At the south end of the bay on its littoral are thousands of acres of salt marshes. Flying over the colored mosaic of seawater confined by levees, one sees the quantities of commercial salt, which are produced by evaporation. These thousands of acres were once used by the Indians. Ancient oyster beds now too polluted for human consumption are sucked up and used for lime in cement plants.

Sail beneath the Golden Gate Bridge spanning the entrance to the bay. Toss a penny into the water to insure your return according to a lenged. Or fly over it and wave *hasta la vista.* You are heading westward around the World, in Focus.

Time: Sundown and after total darkness
Direction: West by southwest
Lens: Moderate wide angle — normal

There are a few moments at sundown when the last of daylight is in balance with the artificial lights of the city. A meter reading of the sky at this time can be used for the first exposure with bracketing for effect. Carried one stop further, one can wait another thirty minutes in mid-latitude areas such as this for near total darkness and make a second exposure for more luminous effect of the city lights, car headlights and taillights, and so forth. Be SURE the camera remains absolutely stationary during the interval.

Lumahai Beach / Kauai, Hawaii

IS THERE A MORE ALLURING SETTING ANYWHERE IN THE WORLD than a white sand beach, clear blue sea and tropical vegetation? Lumahai Beach on the island of Kauai qualifies in the top bracket. Kauai is the greenest, the wettest and the oldest as well as the most eroded island of the archipelago we know as the Hawaiian Islands.

The most isolated land mass in the Pacific, the Hawaiian Islands extend from Midway Island in the mid-Pacific south and eastward to the island called Hawaii at the extreme eastern end of the chain. Our forty-ninth state stretches for 1600 miles from end to end, yet if squeezed together the land mass would be no larger than Connecticut.

When we refer to Hawaii, we mean the Hawaiian Islands, especially the eight volcanic islands which are inhabited by man. The thousands of coral islands and atolls which stretch 1200 miles northwest beyond this group are inhabited almost entirely by millions of feathered creatures — birds, birds and more birds.

This primordial island of Kauai has the distinction of being the number one landfall of the English Captain James Cook in 1778 who, in his devotion to his country, most inappropriately named this group of purely Polynesian islands the Sandwich Islands, in honor of Britain's first Lord of the Admiralty, the Earl of Sandwich. As is well known, Captain Cook was later killed in the Hawaiian Islands.

Lumahai Beach on the north side of the island of Kauai is near a large colonial hotel, the Plantation, which accommodated some of the movie entourage that used this beach in filming *South Pacific*. "Washing that man right out of her hair" on this spot has forever put Lumahai Beach on the pages of theatrical history.

Kauai's superabundance of rainfall — averaging 407 inches a year — makes this the "wettest spot on earth." Waimea Canyon on Kauai has been compared with the Grand Canyon of Arizona — with variations. But gazing into its 3000 feet of depth while feeling secure on the rim does not give you the vertiginous sensation that 5000 feet of sheer rock dropoff produces in the pit of your stomach when standing on the rim of the Grand Canyon. Possibly the vegetation in Waimea Canyon softens the blow — for it is a magnificent sight and colorful.

Time: Midmorning
Direction: West
Lens: Normal

Most photographers and others who take the trip to Kauai agree that this is the most picturesque island. I not only agree but add that I feel this is the world's most beautiful beach from a photogenic viewpoint. There are numerous opportunities for effective framing — changes in wave pattern and lighting conditions. The time of day mentioned happens to be the time when the picture shown here was made. This is not necessarily the only time possible, nor the best time. Weather, location and other factors can make the timing choices rather limited. Often one must be ready after a long period of waiting to obtain any sunlight at all. On other occasions, depending upon the time of day or year, weather and other factors are more predictable and the right time can be chosen.

Waikiki Beach / Oahu, Hawaii

WEATHER IS THE MOST EXPANSIVE SUBJECT OF CONVERSAtion in the world. In the Hawaiian Islands where there is little variation of temperature no one can conscientiously grouse about it no matter what the meteorological situation may be. Too many superlatives have been used to describe our forty-ninth state, but having been in many South Pacific Islands, native and otherwise, the Hawaiian Islands are to us the most lush, meaning a combination of scenic beauty plus luxurious personal comfort.

Waikiki — a perfect stage setting: two miles of white sand beach, palms and a spectacular backdrop — Diamond Head, an extinct volcano. The scene is permanent. The actors are itinerants. Sand has been brought in by barge or truck over a period of years to build and extend the beach. It must be replenished after severe storms which wash it to sea. Humanity in full abandon exhibits itself on Waikiki Beach daily.

Binoculars with a built-in right-angle viewfinder would be a bonanza for a beach vendor at Waikiki. Females could then unabashedly watch a male whose lean rib cage and bird-like neck are being oil-basted on the hour and baked under the tropical sun; or lying next to him supine a Midas-rich baldheaded dotard with a protruding paunch. A budding youth with a twinge of a beard may pass by in contrast to a large handsome Indian Sikh, his long beard carefully combed and smoothed around his face from ear to ear, ends secured under his turban. Also with this cockeyed viewfinder males could relish the array of an equally gossip-inducing group of females ranging from those with steatopygic rears to curvaceous beach bunnies fully aware of their own charms and perfect proportions. One wonders what has become of the old body beautiful — the Venus de Milo type.

Whether you are spending your time looking at the delicious or less appetizing jetsam of the beach, or gazing seaward to the handsome human flotsam riding the surf "hanging ten," there is never a lack of sights, active or dormant. More conservative souls may safely participate in less strenuous outrigger fun, dipping a paddle to Hawaiian rhythm with a group riding in on the surf. A twin-hulled catamaran with billowing red and blue sails and a Hawaiian helmsman will give you a chance to look at Waikiki from the sea.

Like Hawaii itself, Waikiki Beach is a mad mixture of races. Shortly after daylight, an early riser will find the professional beachcomber busy with his modern detection device recovering lost coins and small articles from the sand dropped by the *sans souci* beach sitters and bathers of the previous day.

Many travelers who have spent their holidays *only* on Waikiki Beach say they "have seen Hawaii." In praise of our Aloha State, let it be said they have no more seen the real Hawaii than have travelers who have been only to Delhi or Bombay "seen India."

Time: Midafternoon
Direction: South-southwest
Lens: Normal

Such a scene may or may not suggest one of the world's most photogenic places. It is, however, colorful and lends itself to good composition. Exposure is quite a bit less than normal due to subject brightness. There are numerous vantage points and if one objects to masses of people, they all disappear about five o'clock when late evening light is even more colorful.

Cook's Bay / Moorea, Tahiti

TAHITI IS A SINGLE ISLAND BUT IT HAS BECOME A BLANKET term for all of the Society Islands in French Oceania. Moorea, the beautiful little step-sister of Tahiti, was overlooked by travelers for many years. Indeed, before World War II, Tahiti itself only received occasional steamers and visitors. The non-native living there before World War II was often escaping from life in an overcivilized world.

A comparison of Captain Cook's impressions on his first voyage to Tahiti in 1769 with the glamorous impressions obtained today from tourist folders — tawny-skinned *vahines,* ukuleles, guitars, exotic food, beaches and carefree living — leaves a wide gap. Two hundred years ago Captain Cook praised the geological and botanical features of Tahiti, but wasted few complimentary words on its inhabitants who "make human sacrifices . . . anoint their heads with rancid coconut oil . . . eat lice which they carry with them . . . have neither the spirit nor activity of other natives . . . have only two instruments, the flute and drum."

The atmosphere of romance today which lures the modern traveler here has obviously improved in two centuries. Let's face it! The mere name Tahiti, that so-called Paradise on Earth, fires a bit of the libertine in all of us, male or female. Yet, if you stay long enough you will find some thorns in this paradise, even as in the original one.

Crossing the twelve-mile stretch of water between Tahiti and Moorea, we chug slowly through the narrow opening in the coral reef surrounding Moorea and into a placid green-blue lagoon, thence around to the north side of the island and into the inlet called Cook's Bay. Even anticipating the ultra-ultra in beauty, we are silenced by the dramatic background of two sharp, green volcanic peaks which rise like flattened needles against the cloud-studded sky at the end of the bay. In this miniature tropical fiord, the Tahitian *vahine* in her bright *pareu* and small brother are lifting their narrow *pirogue* into the water. They will paddle their outrigger to the fringes of the bay to fossick on the skeletal coral reef, rummaging for blue starfish, purple sea urchins, cowrie shells and sea anemones.

Time: Early morning
Direction: South
Lens: Normal

Weather often is the factor governing the time of day a photograph can be made. I feel certain that good light exists through sundown for a typical recording of this beautiful little harbor. For me, however, the sun appeared but once, about 8:30 A.M., on one of several days of waiting, yet the rising clouds make a satisfying scene. Humidity might be a factor to consider here on a long visit. Keep film sealed and as dry as possible.

Spear Fisherman / Korolevu Beach, Fiji

THAT THIS HANDSOME CAREFREE FIJIAN SPEAR FISHERMAN is a descendant of a once-cannibalistic tribe — and not too long ago — is as hard to believe as the canary swallowing the cat. This seems to be putting the Fijian's worst foot forward, for today the islanders are peaceful citizens of the British Crown Colony established in 1874. The London Missionary Society in 1835, plus the British law later, put an end to this untidy practice of human steaks. The Fijians were a fighting people and considered their victims a tasty reward of victory. Captain Cook, who lost two of his men to the cook pot on a trip here, also misunderstood the name of the main island, Viti Levu, and interpreted Viti as Fiji.

Large features, black skin and stacks of curly, wiry black hair characterize these Melanesians — *not* Polynesians. The women increase their already-tall stature by wearing their hair high on their heads. But the Fijian man today wears his cut relatively short. For years they were known to travelers as the Fuzzy-wuzzies due to their "crowning glory."

The Fijians, being content with the amount of the world's goods they have, do not make aggressive laborers in the sugar-cane fields nor do they wish to be troubled with business or commerce. East Indians who were brought here by the British in 1877 carry the burden of industry and agriculture. Fijians prefer to fish, to dance and sing to their tom-toms, and to cling to their customs which do not require an extension of effort. Spearfishing in the lagoon near Korolevu Beach on the island of Viti Levu is a customary pastime for the Fijian. If his spear hits the target, the bright red and white *lava lava* will be dropped as he plunges into the seawater to rescue his spear and collect his catch.

In Fiji the *lava lava* is also called a *sula,* especially when worn as a uniform by the police. *Pareu* in Tahiti, *lava lava* in Samoa, *sula* in Fiji, *sarong* in Indonesia — all are a straight piece of cloth donned in slightly different fashion.

Prowling at night with a lantern on the coral reef fringing Viti Levu is more exciting than rubbing Aladdin's lantern for results. When the tide is out the skeletal coral reef is exposed except for a thin veil of seawater covering it. The reef is a limestone formation — the boneyard of coral skeletons. The coral is sharp and can cause nasty cuts, but with proper footwear a traveler can have a rare experience fossicking. Turn over a bright blue starfish and watch it wrap itself in its own arms to recover normal position. Pry loose another eight-armed green starfish with spines and he will roll himself up like a porcupine ball and drift away in the water. You will find black sea slugs (*bêche de mer*), small cowries, sea snails with trap doors called "cats-eyes" (used for jewelry), and even some living brown brain coral. A brilliant small sea snake dashes out of his hole when probed and skims over the surface like a hydrofoil. Along the shoreline tiny octopi hide in sandy holes with the tips of their dainty arms extended.

Who can blame the Fijian for enjoying the sea and its treasures more than the wheels of industry?

Time: Late afternoon
Direction: South
Lens: Normal

Fiji has numerous beautiful beaches, and palm trees along its shores, yet they are not quite comparable to some in Hawaii. For this reason, I felt a combination of the sea and the handsome Fijian fisherman portrayed a more honest picture of this pleasant island's photogenic possibilities. No unusual photographic problems were involved. Courtesy, a small cash payment and a sign of appreciation are all that are required for the model.

Mt. Tasman / Mt. Cook National Park, New Zealand

A N ALP IS JUST A LOFTY MOUNTAIN, BUT THE GREAT WHITE backbone of alps which extends 480 miles in length down the west coast of New Zealand's South Island provides the traveler with a transcendental experience. New Zealand's Southern Alps are a classic in nature's categories.

Although Mt. Cook is the highest of the peaks in this folded mountain range, nearby Tasman, 11,467 feet, is another "cloud piercer" that also provides a magnificent glacier. It is possible to reach the top of Tasman glacier from Ball Hut by a small ski-equipped plane. This literal ski pilot gives his passengers an aerial view of many high peaks, snow fields and glaciers in hanging valleys or on the faces of cliffs. These are unlike the mighty Tasman Glacier which moves relentlessly down a valley for eighteen miles.

Dropping lightly on a snow field at the top of the glacier, the pilot tosses out a snow anchor to keep the plane from carrouselling in the wind and you step out onto the snow-covered ice basin at 8000 feet altitude that is the source of Tasman Glacier. This river of ice, one and a quarter miles wide, is moving towards the Tasman Sea at the rate of about 18 inches a day. Fortunately, there are not great crevasses in this glacier, but ice hummocks are obstacles to worry the tenderfoot when traversing it.

Glaciers are formed when partially melted snow in the high mountain areas compacts into solid ice. This ice is like a viscous or thick fluid and moves gradually down the mountainside or valley, moving more rapidly as it nears the river or sea at its base. Since it melts faster at its base — where it is also moving faster — great frozen masses often break from the glacier and plunge thunderously into the sea.

The Dutchman Abel Tasman, for whom the mountain was named, saw the Southern Alps from the sea in 1642 but was influenced not to make a landfall here by the cannibalistic tribesmen whose home it was. He gave the island a Dutch name that was later changed to New Zealand, also Dutch.

Sir Edward Hillary, a native of New Zealand — a Kiwi — who interestingly was a beekeeper as a young man, has conditioned himself for some of the world's most rugged mountain climbing in the Southern Alps of his own country. You may abhor mountain climbing per se, but if you carry your skis with you in the plane to the top of Tasman Glacier, you can enjoy an exciting downhill run alongside the glacier back to Ball Hut from where you took off.

Time: Midday
Direction: Northwest
Lens: Normal

Though this beautiful mountain can be photographed from several vantage points reached by car or on foot, this is one place where an aerial photograph can be far more advantageous. And here air service is available a few yards from the government hotel — the Hermitage — at the base of the glacier. If the windows of the plane are clean one can photograph the mountain quite easily — I suggest a rather fast shutter speed. Snow exposure is quite difficult to judge when using a meter due to the snow's high reflectivity. I usually use the equivalent of one stop smaller aperture than my basic normal exposure for an average subject.

Milford Sound / New Zealand

MILFORD SOUND IS SOUTH OF MT. COOK IN NEW ZEALAND'S west coastal area of beautiful fiords. There is a tendency for travelers to compare the fiords of New Zealand with those of Norway — both are spellbinding. But beyond their qualities of rare beauty, there is nothing really comparable.

Norway was once an ice-capped country; New Zealand, of volcanic origin, never lay beneath the great ice cap. Norway is on the fringe of the Arctic; New Zealand is the jumping-off place for the Antarctic Continent. The early inhabitants of Norway were Teutons while the New Zealand primitives were Polynesians. The Nordic word for these deep inlets of the sea was *vik,* a sheltered cove from which the Norse Vikings ambushed passing ships. This is entirely inapplicable to New Zealand for its fiords are not even now used commercially. Geologists largely favor the theory that the fiords in both countries were carved by glaciers, leaving deep inlets to be inundated by the seawater.

Milford Sound with its blue depths equal to the height of its sheer towering walls, is pure delight. From the Government Hotel with its neat New Zealand flowerbeds, you look upon Mitre Peak. A bishop's cap is the most fitting name for this peak — a mitre.

After Abel Tasman had seen New Zealand in 1642 and gone his way, the next explorer on record is Captain Cook who, in 1769, arrived on the first of his three expeditions to the Pacific. He charted the coasts of New Zealand and gave names to many places, not forgetting the name Cook which was attached to the most outstanding features of the country — Mt. Cook, and Cook Straits that separate the north and south islands of New Zealand. We seem to keep tripping over this gritty navigator and explorer throughout the early history of the Pacific. It is well to give him due honor and credit for having charted this great unknown area of the Pacific as well as many other areas, laying foundations from which the whole world has profited. There is no explorer like unto Cook today.

Time: Early morning
Direction: West
Lens: Normal — moderate wide angle

Normal camera procedure and average exposure are all that are required. Here a combination of man's gardening and nature's wonders work together for a magnificent scene — yet an obvious wire, perhaps an aerial for radio reception, has been stretched in front of this great attraction (and retouched out of this picture). I am continually disappointed by the seeming disinterest in retaining the naturalness of scenery. Wires, transmission lines and poles, signs and buildings are being thoughtlessly placed in line with many of the most beautiful sights of nature, sights that have in the past thrilled thousands.

Harbor with Coathanger Bridge / Sydney, Australia

THE COLLOQUIAL NAME "COATHANGER" WHICH HAS BEEN attached to this great single span steel arch bridge over Sydney Harbor is so obvious that it needs no explanation. Using the principle of the Roman arch, steel arch bridges are not uncommon throughout the world, but the "Coathanger" built in 1932 is one of the largest. Under its span the largest ships afloat can pass.

Sydney Harbor perfectly exemplifies the definition of a harbor as "a sheltered place to provide protection for ships." After you have sailed between the two Heads (high sandstone cliffs separated by three-quarters of a mile of sea) which form the entrance to Sydney Harbor, there is a sense of calm security on its deep blue waters. There is no "in" nor "out" other than this narrow gateway.

As Captain Cook sailed by it in 1770 he named this harbor Port Jackson for the Secretary of the British Admiralty. Ingratiating himself with the members of the Admiralty by bestowing their names upon his discoveries seems to have become a habit with Cook. However, Botany Bay, fourteen miles south of Port Jackson which Cook discovered and where he found uncooperative Aborigines with their spears and *woomeras* rampant, was given the name Botany because of the many botanical varieties found there. It was later, in 1788, that Governor Arthur Phillips landed his shiploads of British prisoners — largely political — within the magnificent Port Jackson harbor and established the city of Sydney Cove.

There are beautiful homes today on the shores of its many fronds or inlets, and on the shores bordering the bay in the center of the city are docks and commercial establishments. From a penal colony Sydney has grown to be a thriving industrial and suburban city of substantial citizens.

Australia has become a progressive self-governing nation of the British Commonwealth, a country of great opportunity and potentiality. The largest island and the smallest continent in the world, it is about six times the size of India. According to Cook it was "an empty and barren land except for kangaroos." Little did he realize that its kangaroos and many other marsupials found only in Australia make it unlike any other continent.

Marco Polo laid claim to having seen Australia as did the French but unquestionably the Dutch were the first Europeans to set foot upon it, in 1606. There is good evidence that they explored the north and west coasts of Australia but called it New Holland. The name has mutated through New Holland, New South Wales, and Terra Australis to Australia. But the first authentic colony was established by the British in Sydney Harbor.

Time: Past sundown
Direction: North
Lens: Normal to long

Like the Bay Bridge of San Francisco, Coathanger Bridge with its evening lights is a man-made attraction symbolizing a city. Within the area, opportunities for photographs of natural beauty abound, due to Sydney's magnificent harbor and land contour. Again, this is a photograph made at the dusk period when the sky light is close in exposure value to that of the city's lights. By waiting longer with shutter closed one can make a second exposure for the lights alone, including those of autos, ships, and windows.

The Ginza / Tokyo, Japan

GINZA! THE NAME IS ECUMENICAL, UNIVERSAL! THE GINZA is both a street and an area in the world's largest city in the land of the Rising Sun. The Ginza is only eight blocks long, but it is eight blocks of dynamite both by day and night. A street that had its origin as a quiet way where the coin of the realm was minted and stored (*gin* = silver, *za* = association) has transformed itself completely. Here and now there is a frenetic spending of silver in the shops, specialty stores, department stores, restaurants, bars, liquor stores, night clubs, movies and theatres. Floor space in this crowded real estate is at such a premium that rental figures are unquotable and still soaring.

Chuo Chuo is the real name of this street, which if you look you may find on the street sign post, but who ever heard of it? When the cherry trees died out they were replaced by weeping willows. The living willows, however, do not preclude the use of artificial cherry blossoms to decorate the shops and streets of Tokyo during the spring months.

By day you notice the *noren,* banners or curtains which hang in front of shops and stores with the insignia or symbol of the owner emblazoned thereon — a Japanese type of coat-of-arms. If you are searching for a liquor store, look for a straw rope, a *nawa noren,* hanging outside the shop to identify it. The word *noren* also means "reputation of face." The great department stores display huge *noren* — their honorable "face-flags."

In the midst of murderous traffic on the Ginza, you may still see an occasional rickshaw, a *gin-bur* toting a geisha to work at her teahouse. Modern office girls often wear the uniform of their employers and bounce along the Ginza chattering on their way to a coffee break or luncheon. In the midst of sellers-of-everything, you may find a modern wedding hall where a Shinto marriage is performed. With modern young Japanese the Shinto Shrine as a wedding chapel is taking second place to these halls. Japanese hairdressers are also open for business along the Ginza. These *mage* shops offer specific styles for women in different occupations — be it housewife, office girl or geisha. Restaurants on the Ginza are cosmopolitan with menus running the gamut from tempura to tenderloin. A new post-war section, the Nishi-Ginza, is now included in the vague boundaries of the Ginza.

Nocturnal activities, movies, dinner, shows, night clubs, start at an early hour — 5:30 P.M. — since by government law night clubs must stop serving food and drinks by 11:30 P.M. As usual, there are exceptions to this restriction since "supper clubs" may function until 5:00 A.M. This partial "curfew" may reduce the large number of traffic accidents at night; also it gives a good night of sleep to the Japanese who are early to work as well as the tourist with a "big day of sightseeing tomorrow."

Time: Dusk
Direction: East
Lens: Moderate wide angle

Multiple exposure can be used if sky is of importance. However, this is a typical example of a situation where a meter reading of sky and artificial light can be used to balance the two exposure problems. A period of up to ten minutes exists when a long exposure can be made to record both conditions as well as car lights. I have included this scene more for its unusualness in the Far East than for its beauty as it is more typical of Times Square than Japan.

Yomeimon Gate / Toshogu Shrine—Nikko, Japan

W E ONCE ASKED A POST-WORLD WAR II JAPANESE STUDENT who claimed he was an agnostic to tell us the difference between Shintoism and Buddhism as he saw it. His foggy reply was, "Well, Shintoism is connected with birth and marriages and happiness; Buddhism has more to do with death."

The tenets of both Shintoism and Buddhism are deeply involved in Japanese worship. "The Shinto Gods' world is one of the most complicated to be found in the entire history of religion." We have seen children brought to the Shinto shrines for dedication and have also seen marriages there. We have watched worshipers in prayerful attitude stand before the front grating of the Shinto shrine, ring bells, clap their hands to attract the deities' attention and toss their paper prayers through the grating hopefully.

There is gaiety in the sacred dancing girls of the Shinto shrine and there is color — always the red oxide of lead which produces that vermillion color peculiar to the Shinto shrine only, in distinct contrast to the solemn monastic gray of the Buddhist temple. Like a Japanese home there is simplicity of architecture in the shrine. The Chinese curved roof lines were added after the introduction of Buddhism into Japan. There are no images or idols in a Shinto shrine.

On the other hand, the Buddhist temple is a heavy, timbered building, its exterior weathered gray, and its roof of smoked gray tiles. There are usually many images of Buddha within a Buddhist temple as well as guardian demons. It is not uncommon to enter a Buddhist temple and find a large group of Buddhist priests praying for a departed ancestor or intoning the merits of Buddha.

The Toshogu Shrine, built during the dynasty of the Tokugawa Shoguns is a potpourri, an amalgamation of both religions. Japan's native Shintoism had its basis in worship of the Emperor as a divine being. When a Buddhist temple was erected beside a Shinto shrine in Nikko in 716 A.D., the invading Buddhist hierarchy was astute enough to deify the Emperor as "the great incarnation of Buddha, the light of the East."

There are so many apparent conflicting beliefs in the two religions that it is difficult to understand how the Japanese can embrace them both. Perhaps it is a case of complementarity. The Toshogu Shrine is so effusive in its details that it is bewildering. A purely lovely aspect of this ornate shrine, however, is a long double row of cryptomeria trees — evergreens over 300 years old — stretching for twenty-five miles in stately grandeur and leading to the gates of this shrine.

Once you enter this elaboration of temples, shrines, toriis, gateways, ablution fountains, royal stable — all completely smothered with carvings or decorative art, dragons and flowers, mythical creatures, animals in gold and color — you are seized by a feeling of unreality.

In a lower courtyard is the famous carved trio of monkeys, deaf, dumb and blind to evil. At the top of the third flight of stone steps you face the Yomeimon Gate, too cluttered to describe. There is one pillar here which puts you in reverse gear for a moment, for the carved figures are standing on their heads in order to cast out and remove fear from this area. This shrine was built by the first Shogun of the Tokugawa family. More accurately it was built by 15,000 laborers for the Shogun's pleasure.

Time: Midmorning
Direction: Northeast
Lens: Wide angle

High-contrast subjects are quite difficult to photograph. Overhanging roofs shade detailed carvings. Local Japanese photographers use large silvered reflectors for added shadow lighting. One problem encountered here was continual groups of black-clad students on vacation tours. Almost all had cameras, and by the time the three-hour procession had passed the sun was quite high. Few Japanese had ever seen a camera larger than a 35mm, and our large 5 x 7" Linhof created as much interest as the shrines.

Dokuza Tei Garden / Kyoto, Japan

PEACE, REPOSE, RESTRAINT, SIMPLICITY, DELICACY, WITH-drawal! These are qualities which the occidental enjoys in an oriental garden. The Japanese seem prenatally endowed with insight into the symbolism and ideology of Japanese gardens which are only superficially understood by westerners. In Kyoto there are several Zen Buddhist temples and gardens such as this one.

In ancient days Zen Buddhist monks were masters of art, painting and literature. Later, in the 1500s, they translated the Chinese black and white landscape paintings into three-dimensional form, creating the dry-landscape garden called *karesansui*. An illusion of moving water is produced by the swirling rake marks in the sandy gravel. There is no water in a dry-landscape garden, no pond, no waterfall. Stones play the most important role. Originally fifteen stones were used in a Zen garden and each stone bore a Buddhistic name. The austerity of the garden is in keeping with the seclusion sought by Zen priests for their meditation to attain enlightenment.

Japanese gardens *(shin-gyo-so* — elaborate, not so elaborate or abbreviated) are either artificial hills or level gardens. They are classified as *ryoan-ji,* dry landscapes such as the Zen Buddhists build. They may be *roji,* the highly specialized stepping-stone garden of the tea house where one also finds stone basins and lanterns.

Rotating gardens, *kaiyu,* where one can wander savoring the pools, ponds, waterfalls, bridges, shrubbery, evergreens and a few blossoms, are the gardens dear to the hearts of travelers from the Western Hemisphere for here is familiarity. *Shakkei* gardens, "landscape borrowed and drawn into a garden setting," have become popularized by modern architects and have been incorporated in modern buildings. There is one in the Sky Room of Tokyo's Nikko Hotel.

A Japanese authority says "the Japanese have conquered nature by overcoming 'natural nature' with 'artificial nature.'" This sounds a bit like doubletalk to the westerner ignorant of and untrained in the subtleties of Japanese gardens. But it does not preclude his keen enjoyment of them.

Time: Morning
Direction: South — overcast light
Lens: Wide angle

The simplicity of Japanese gardens lends itself to uncluttered and well-composed photographs. With such a subject cloudy weather doesn't necessarily make the scene any less interesting though more contrasting lighting could emphasize the raked gravel. The light-colored stones dominate the exposure reading, so slightly favor the darker areas, though flat light makes exposure quite easy. Permission is required and is given freely. Shoes must be removed.

Heian Shrine Garden / Kyoto, Japan

IN THE SPAN OF MAN'S TIME ON EARTH THERE HAVE ALWAYS been gardens, beginning with Eden. The first gardens were sources of food, followed by herb gardens for medicine. In logical succession came the gardens of aesthetic beauty. The ancient empires of the world, Babylonia, Egypt, Persia and succeeding ones, all had gardens with their own traditional characteristics.

Buddhist monks carried the idea of gardens into China where the wealthy indulged in them. The poorer Chinese, without enough land for a full-size garden, built miniature gardens, dwarfing trees and shrubs in ratio to the size of the garden. Lacking *any* garden space, they made mini-miniature gardens within bowls. Buddhist missionaries brought Chinese gardens to Japan. Today the creation of a Japanese garden, no matter what kind, is a highly developed art. The Heian Shrine Garden in Kyoto is one that travelers are not apt to miss. There is a soft and delicate charm here which is missing in the stern ascetic gardens of the Zen Buddhists.

In 1895, when the present Heian Shrine was built as a replica of Kyoto's former Imperial Palace — 1000 years ago — this garden was developed. The pond, the Blue Dragon Pool, is crossed by a studied arrangement of steppingstones which is known as the Sleeping Dragon Bridge. These round stones, like lily pads, were a later addition to the garden, being cross sections of stone pillars from an ancient abandoned bridge. The Japanese call the Heian Shrine Garden a *kaiyu* — a rotating garden — which we would translate as a "sauntering garden."

Time: Afternoon
Direction: South
Lens: Normal

Overcast lighting often gives a soft feeling to such objects — actually bringing out detail that would be lost in bright sunlight. Exposure was by direct meter reading. The main obstacle was the hundreds of people wanting to try their skill crossing over the stones. Finally, a tour guide saw my predicament and held up traffic for a few minutes. Japanese courtesy is in evidence in almost every encounter.

Torii at Miyajima Shrine / Japan

ON AN ARM OF JAPAN'S INLAND SEA OF SETO, NOT FAR FROM Hiroshima, is the sacred island of Miyajima. Its elaborate torii appears to rise and sink out of the tide waters of the bay in bogus reality. The Torii of Miyajima is almost as famous as Japan's mountain, Fuji-san.

Toriis were first built as simple bird roosts, two uprights and a cross bar. In the evolution of torii architecture many of them have become complicated and ornate. This torii which stands in front of the sacred Shinto Shrine Itsukushima on the island of Miyajima, shimmers when reflected in the still waters beneath it — an apparition. It was constructed of camphorwood in 1875 and stands rooted in the sea.

A torii is always associated with a Shinto Shrine, never a Buddhist temple, unless the two are intermixed in a temple grounds. But the sacred shrine of Itsukushima is purely Shinto, Japan's "blood-bone" religion centuries before Buddhism was introduced from China. Itsukushima Shrine, more extensive than the usual Shinto shrine, dates back to 811 A.D. There have been several restorations of this wooden building which is built on posts and overhangs the water's edge in brilliant splendor.

Pilgrims come daily to the island of Miyajima but arrive in hordes when the special yearly festival is held here. It is quite simple for the visitor to reach the island by car and ferry boat from Hiroshima. On hot days awnings are stretched across the neat streets of the town under which you can saunter comfortably and windowshop or buy a Japanese meal. For that matter you can buy a cash-and-carry-out Japanese meal neatly packed in a red lacquer box.

A "law" forbids one to be born or to die on Miyajima since either would contaminate this sacred island — particularly death which is considered a pollution. But since man controls neither of these functions there have undoubtedly been infractions of this law. And how can anyone punish the infraction of death?

Time: Afternoon
Direction: Northwest
Lens: Normal

Several views of the Torii are possible with morning or afternoon framing through the pines. At low tide it is possible to approach much closer. At frequent intervals a shrine priest, dressed in a brilliant red costume, dances for the visitors. Nearby is a five-storied pagoda.

Rice Terraces / Banaue, Philippines

IN LUZON, THE NORTH ISLAND OF THE PHILIPPINE REPUBLIC, 4000 feet above sea level at Banaue, live the Ifugaos, a subtribe of the Igorots. The Ifugaos wear only a G-string and for centuries were head-hunters. The head-lopping habit ceased under the persuasion of the United States government in 1898, but the G-string remains the man's attire while the Ifugao women modestly sport a *tapis* or skirt.

It is anomalous that these primitive tribesmen whose belief is animism, are also remarkable engineers. Their sinuous, tiered rice terraces carved from the raw mountainside with only wooden tools, over a 2000-year period, are considered one of the Orient's great engineering achievements. Walls of rock and clay, some of them over fifty feet high, were built to form land pockets of about 100,000 acres which are their arable rice fields. Originally taro and millet were grown in these sculptured paddies.

Ifugao women plant rice seeds in December in solidly compacted rice nurseries. By February and March the rice is large enough for them to transplant into the paddies. Heavy rains in June supplement the irrigation during the long growing season, for the rice is not harvested until August. Rains fall again during the succeeding months between harvest and December, completing the yearly cycle. Every stalk of rice is planted, weeded and harvested by hand and only the women work on the terraces. The men tend the babies and once a year clean weeds from the terrace walls. Their responsibility is also to see that the irrigation system functions.

From the top of the cordillera, water is channeled through bamboo pipes and drops from one terrace to the next one beneath it. Silt and organic material carried by the dropping water plus straw are the only fertilizers. No manure or chemicals are used, because three species of fish living in the flooded terraces would die if these fertilizers were applied. A few of the Ifugaos now use insecticides but in such cases the water must be piped away from the fields below them.

An outsider cannot purchase rice, rice wine or a field of rice. To the natives belongs the rice crop *(palay)* and yet this can supply only 40 percent of their own needs. Sturdy young Ifugao men have overdeveloped leg and thigh muscles from their hillside stances. By middle age the men have seamy faces, gnarled bodies and rheumy eyes caused by the smoke of the cook pot in their primitive huts. Betel nut, the oriental's chewing gum, which causes copious salivation, leaves red mouths, lips and brown teeth.

One stands in awe as he looks upon these rice terraces, wave upon wave of them, the work of primitive people in the heat and humidity of the tropics. Spotted here and there in the green fields a brilliant red plant appears. It is not a weed. Like our roadside cross, it marks the spot of the violent death of a human being.

The Banaue rice terraces, cached away in the northern Philippines are not recommended for "dear hearts and gentle people." It takes fortitude, patience and endurance to reach them — guts. So Ray Manley brings them to *you*.

Time: Early morning
Direction: Southeast
Lens: Normal

Weather can determine your choice of time though both morning and afternoon light could be used. Because northern Luzon is quite mountainous, rainfall is quite heavy even in the dry period of March and April. The earth and green rice terraces here are quite dark and their correct exposure is essential. Avoid reading the brilliant light of the clouds. The area is reached by a long drive from Baguio, which is an hour from Manila by plane. This is probably one of the more off-the-beaten-path areas represented in this book — yet it is truly one of the wonders of the world and well worth seeing.

Mount Mayon Volcano / Luzon, Philippines

HAD VULCAN (VOLCANUS), THE ROMAN MYTHICAL GOD of Fire, ever existed, he would have been pleased with nature's profligate display of his namesakes — volcanoes — throughout the world. The area encompassing the Pacific Ocean and often called "the circle of fire" has produced many volcanic peaks erupted from earth's hot interior. Among them, Mt. Shasta, Mt. Osorno and Fuji-san are beautiful symmetrical cones, often snow-covered. However, Mt. Mayon — roundly 8000 feet high — near the town of Legaspi and the end of the peninsula extending southeast of Manila on Luzon, is claimed to be "the perfect cone."

Mt. Mayon still snores enough and emits enough hot breath to make one aware that it is only dormant. It is honest. But this does not deter people from enjoying health resorts built on its bubbling slopes where its blisters are called hot springs. It has always mystified me why man will return and rebuild in areas where unpredictable volcanoes have erased whole populations. "Nestling" in a resort on the side of an active volcano has as much lure as shaking hands with a striking rattlesnake.

On the plus side such a cone as this has majesty, power and beauty. Also, the lava and ash which it spews out becomes, centuries later, fertile soil where crops like *abaca* (manila hemp) and coconuts are grown.

A great eruption here in 1815 caused many deaths and much damage. Again in 1897 Mt. Mayon blew its bonnet. Even vulcanologists do not presume to set a date for its next "hat-doffing." Apparently undisturbed, the town of Legaspi sits at the base of Mt. Mayon enjoying its reputation as the commercial center of south Luzon.

The Spaniards were the first Europeans to find the Philippine Islands, 700 of them more or less, and named them for their King Philip II. The fifth Spanish expedition was led by Miguel Lopez de Legazpi for whom the town was named by Americans in 1925. Its former name was Albay.

Kilroy was in Legaspi in World War II and left his usual trademark painted on the sea wall of Legaspi where it will probably remain until obliterated by wind, water or Mt. Mayon.

Time: Early morning
Direction: North
Lens: Normal

This active volcano and its proximity to Legaspi's photogenic harbor lends itself to an interesting general view. A hill of a few hundred feet in height lies south of the harbor, and is an ideal vantage point. Walking through the stilted houses along the beach is in itself a never-to-be-forgotten experience. Exposure presents no problem but haze from burning fields seems to subside overnight with clearer air before noon.

Hong Kong Harbor (Fragrant Harbor)

HONG KONG HARBOR — KNOWN ON MAPS AS VICTORIA Harbor — is not a bay but a roadstead, a strip of water between the island of Hong Kong and the city of Kowloon opposite on the China mainland.

About 125 years ago when Captain Elliot, R. N., first occupied the island of Hong Kong for the British, the flickering flame of peanut oil lamps glowed here. Kerosene lamps flared by 1857. Gas was introduced for light and cooking (no house heating needed) in 1861, and finally in 1889 electricity blazed its way through the island. Now with the addition of neon lighting Hong Kong Harbor at night has the refulgence of a Disney fantasy. The Chinese translation of Hong Kong is Fragrant Harbor.

By day it is a harbor where 600 ships a month arrive, where Chinese junks and sampans transport local merchandise or unload and load large ships anchored in the harbor. Passenger ferries and *walla wallas* — motor launches — cross and recross from the city of Victoria on the island to the city of Kowloon on the mainland every few minutes. It is a bustling waterway and yet a visitor does not feel bustled in this tropical atmosphere.

There is no bridge across the harbor but ferries of all kinds are efficient and plentiful. Reclaimed land forms an arm into the harbor on the Kowloon side on which was built in 1958 a long runway for the Kai Tak International Airport. Recently a handsome modern Ocean Terminal, also on the Kowloon side, has been erected in which the shops display the products of Hong Kong. Hong Kong is now promoting trade throughout the world.

This Fragrant Harbor is not always one of still waters, in witness of which are two typhoon shelters that are sardine-packed colonies of sampans and junks. Hong Kong has a "permanent floating" population of 150,000 Chinese who spend their entire lives on junks and sampans. Their permanency is obvious, lashed as many of them are thwart to thwart in these typhoon shelters, but the floating seems restricted to a vertical movement, up or down with the 10-to-15-foot tide of the harbor.

"On the 23rd day of the third moon" — spring — the harbor belongs to the Chinese junks and sampans. Even the dwellers of the typhoon shelters break loose and emerge from behind their breakwaters to celebrate the birthday of their protectress, the Mother of Heaven, Tin Hau. The festivities last for four days. Junks and sampans are jammed with celebrants headed for Joss House Bay, nine miles west of Hong Kong where there is an important shrine to Tin Hau. To the outsider witnessing this celebration it is a dream world of lions, dragons, unicorns, paper shrines, brilliant paper flowers, colorful silken banners, joss sticks and firecrackers. There are floats on land and junks on the sea, brilliantly decorated.

Hong Kong Harbor, which early history connects with clipper ships, pirates and opium runners has, within a period of slightly over a century, become not only one of the world's most important harbors economically, but from the human viewpoint probably the most exciting harbor in the world.

It is still a British colony and the address is just HONG KONG.

Time: Sunset
Direction: West
Lens: Long

This is possibly one of the most photogenic large harbors in the world. High vantage points, numerous lights, and its general position make it ideal for overall views both day and night. Night exposure is a bit complicated in that one exposure should be made at sunset, slightly underexposing the sky, yet retaining some detail in the buildings. After total darkness, an exposure of lengthy duration can be made to record the city lights and the lights of the many ferries crossing the smooth water.

Aberdeen / Hong Kong

THE NAME OF THIS AREA, ABERDEEN, WOULD LEAD ONE TO expect a Scottish village whose inhabitants wore tartans and played bagpipes. It is verily at the other end of the rainbow. Aberdeen is the home base of Chinese fishermen called the Dragon People — several Chinese tribes whose language and customs are unrelated to the land-dwelling Chinese of Hong Kong. The name refers to Lord Aberdeen, Britain's Foreign Secretary when Hong Kong was first settled. British "limeys" who came here for fresh water called it "Waterfall Bay."

Long before Captain Elliot claimed Hong Kong for his Queen Victoria, the forefathers of the Dragon People fished in Hong Kong waters. They are still fishermen although some of them have converted their junks into cargo lighters for the large ships which come and go in Hong Kong Harbor. Their fishing junks and sampans nuzzle each other in Aberdeen Harbor which is situated south of Hong Kong, less than a half hour by taxi.

In spite of the lack of cleanliness, there is a magnetic and pictorial quality here which draws many visitors. Small sampans oared or poled by the Dragon women grinning under their inverted basket hats, carry passengers hither and yon. In boarding a sampan you may step over a naked sleeping baby or watch an older child shoveling a bowl of rice into his eager mouth with full-sized chop sticks. The masts of the large junks in the harbor are sail-less and against the sky look like a thousand protruding wooden spikes. Sadly, for the romanticists, sails are disappearing into limbo, being replaced with engines and motors. Fewer and fewer patched or colored sails are unfurled on these clumsy junks.

Just before sundown you may watch some of them moving down the channel of Aberdeen Harbor heading to sea for many days of fishing. Their families are aboard, the weary washing is flapping, the fish nets are dried and ready for action, and invariably a long line of dried fish is suspended like icicles from a line stretched across the high stern of the junk. There is nothing modern in this arrangement except the engine.

Among the many fish and sea creatures for sale on the Aberdeen wharves a visitor is curious about the stiff, dried snakes, coiled realistically as if about to strike. The "barbarian" would not understand so the Dragon People vaguely refer to them as "good medicine for health and love" — aphrodisiacs.

A rather drab harbor viewed in daylight becomes under night's screen a spectrum of colors. The Dragon People have taken advantage of the traveler's curiosity and Hong Kong dollars. Two floating seafood restaurants are anchored among the junks. Ancient lanterns have been supplanted by colored electric lights and neon lighting but the food remains Chinese, from fish lips to duck's feet.

The town of Aberdeen adjoins the harbor on Hong Kong island. Solid rows of old buildings house some of this 150,000 floating population where young families are now in schools, or whose old parents have ceased to be useful at sea. We were welcomed in one of these Chinese homes, 12' x 26' in size, where twenty members of the same family, from great-grandmother to an unborn babe, shared their meager existence. From their only window, Ray Manley photographed Aberdeen Harbor.

Time: Midmorning
Direction: South
Lens: Normal

There are many possibilities in this city of sampans. A high vantage point is needed to show a portion of this overcrowded harbor. A friendly shopkeeper or apartment resident will probably oblige. This will give you a glimpse of the crowded yet well-disciplined and happy home of a family of some twenty adults and children. A daylight view requires only normal procedures, while a dusk exposure can be balanced properly a few moments after sundown.

IF THE FRENCH NATURALIST, HENRI MOUHAT, HAD NOT SPIED the gray pinnacles of the temple of Angkor (Angkor Wat) above the miasmic green jungle of Cambodia where he was poking about for specimens, the treasures of the Khmer civilization might still be embalmed in arboreal wrappings. This event occurred in 1860, over 400 years after this area had been deserted by its builders.

It is claimed that missionaries, those unsung explorers, had seen these ruins in the sixteenth century, but it was French archaeologists and anthropologists after 1860 who were responsible for uncovering these rare monuments.

Who built them, when and why? History is a must here. Without it these ruins are just mysterious masses of carved stone. For more than 600 years, from 790 A.D. to 1432 A.D., Angkor was the flourishing capital of the Cambodian (Kambujan) Khmers. Here they had homes, markets, shops, temples and plenty of rice from their irrigated fields. It was and is a humid land only 10 feet above sea level. This creative yet luxury-loving civilization became decadent and, without strong leadership, it fell in 1432 A.D. under the onslaught of the Thai people. Moving southward under Mongol pressure, the Thais vanquished the Khmers and departed. There is substantial evidence that part of the Thai loot was the living Royal Ballet Corps of the Khmers, the descendants of whom are seen today as the Thai Royal Court Dancers.

Credit as founder of the Khmer kingdom belongs to Jayavarman II who put the first solid building block into this empire in 790 A.D. Near the shores of the great Cambodian lake Tonle Sap, he built the city of Angkor Thom. During his 60-year reign he established boundaries and set up a system of agriculture, government and religion which stood throughout the existence of the Khmer empire. Jayavarman II was powerful enough to have the priests declare him a deity — a King God. The Hindu influence of the Siva cult from India had already penetrated here. This Siva cult, the worship of the phallic image of procreation called the *lingam,* was enshrined in their holy-of-holies as it is even today in Siva temples in India. This cult known as *Devaraja* was continued by the succeeding Khmer monarchs who were also considered man-gods. Buddhism came into Cambodia some centuries later.

A succession of kings with their bickerings and accomplishments followed. Then, in 1113 A.D., Suryavarman II loomed over Khmer affairs, restoring peace and building the incomparable temple of Angkor Wat. As with the other *Devaraja* temples, this temple too had a purposeful end — his own tomb. Breaking tradition, Suryavarman II built his necropolis, Angkor Wat, outside of the city walls.

The visitor is stunned by its massive bulk and at the same time by its delicacy and beauty. Immense sandstones brought, it is said, on bamboo rafts, have been piled and sculptured by true artists. Intricate description of its moats, causeways, galleries and terraces is only confusing to one who has not been *sur place.* Ray Manley's superb photograph of Angkor Wat needs no additional description.

Vivid recollections are of its lotus-topped pinnacles and its powerful proportions. There are contrasts between the strong and delicate of the carvings; and its bas-reliefs picture the Khmer life of the time.

Time: Night
Direction: East
Lens: Normal

The tour directions used in visiting Angkor Wat, Angkor Thom, and others suggest that certain areas be visited in morning light, winding up with the largest — Angkor Wat — in midafternoon. For a view of the great entry to this temple this is quite correct, yet the back portion of the temple also is quite impressive, with more opportunities for framing and an alternate view if cloud formations are better from this direction. Though the temples are black, normal exposure readings can be used except for close-up detail. Unfortunately, during my visit they were burning the rice fields and the sky beyond Angkor Wat was not its customary blue. This circumstance led me to a new approach to the subject which, in its final effect, gives a more colorful rendition. Use a time exposure for artificial lighting after an earlier exposure for the sky. Film should be protected from heat and humidity here as in Bangkok.

Bayon Gateway, Angkor Thom / Siem Reap, Cambodia

JAYAVARMAN VII — SON OF SURYAVARMAN II — CAME TO THE Khmer throne in 1181 A.D. While rebuilding the colossal city of Angkor Thom, his Khmer slaves also constructed his personal temple in the heart of the Thom, the Bayon. This mammoth sandstone agglutination — a mixture of Sivaistic-Buddhistic architecture — was a monument to his egotism. Forty-nine pyramidal towers are built on receding platforms. On each tower are carved four great stone faces, replicas of the King. There is a great similarity in these faces — powerful jaw, square skull, half-closed eyes and inscrutable smile, perhaps a relentless one. Jayavarman VII considered himself wholly divine, a Living Buddha. Today's translation would be a superb megalomaniac.

The entire Bayon is overcrowded with bizarre and detailed sculpturing documenting the domestic life and wars of the Khmers. The montage of 200 almost-identical stone faces zooming in and out of focus as the traveler looks in awe upon them is an indescribable experience.

The Bayon was the final great monument erected in Angkor Thom before the Khmer demise. After the reign of Jayavarman VII, a period of "gorgeous decadence," the Khmer civilization declined. The people were exhausted, tax-burdened, and their slaves were rebellious. The Thai invasion dissipated the kingdom as such. While the ancient capital of Cambodia — Angkor — slid into the arms of the jungle to remain hidden for 400 years, the Khmers have lived on as the Cambodian people. They still speak the Khmer language.

Time: Morning
Direction: South
Lens: Normal

Though the Bayon is the principal temple in the Angkor Thom complex, I found the Gateway quite photogenic, characterized by the four faces of Buddha very much the same as the ninety-six faces at the Bayon itself. Human interest can be added to the scene as an occasional trishaw passes through the gate, having brought a few hardy sightseers the several-mile distance from the nearby hotels. The Bayon can be photographed from all four sides, but I felt the eastern face was the most photogenic. Because there are tall trees in front of the Bayon it is necessary to wait until 9:30 or 10:00 A.M. before the sun strikes the Buddha faces without shadow.

Temple of the Emerald Buddha / Bangkok, Thailand

THE EMERALD BUDDHA ONLY 26 INCHES HIGH? A MERE TRINket you say! On the contrary, this small masterpiece of carved green crystal is the rarest and most revered Buddha in Thailand.

The Temple of the Emerald Buddha — Wat Phra Keo — is the King's own temple. A stone wall encloses the compound within which are the formal gardens and official Palace of the King. Here too are numerous buildings of religious significance — pagodas with spiraled tapered crowns, pagodas of rounded Cambodian architecture, bell towers, and the Temple of the Emerald Buddha. Scattered throughout this Buddhist compound are mythological figures of ogres, magic monkey-gods, the half-man-half-rooster Garuda, cows, Nagas (snakes) and other animals which have roots in both Hinduism and Buddhism. It is a bizarre mixture. For the photographer there is a bewildering amount of riches, particularly when the sun is shining on the glitter of colored enamel roof tiles, the tinkling bells hanging from the temples' eaves and the maze of buildings covered with bright mosaics — broken bits of gay china and gold leaf.

Two giant ogres (Yaks) guard the entrance of the Temple of the Emerald Buddha. In contrast, within the temple the venerated Emerald Buddha seems a miniature, 66 centimeters from its base to the top of the head and mounted high on an altar beneath four jeweled, tiered parasols graduated in size. According to the Director of the Temple of the Emerald Buddha,

"The whole body including its base is made of a single piece of polished dark green crystal somewhat like real emerald."

In August this cherished image was garbed in a golden robe which exposed the head and one green shoulder. When the weather is cooler, only the face of the Buddha is left uncovered. In feverishly hot weather modesty demands only a few wisps of veiling. The King of Thailand provides these rich garments and jewels for his Buddha. There are diverse histories of its origin but it is well authenticated that the Emerald Buddha was brought to Bangkok in 1787 A.D.

Elsewhere among the 300 *wats* or temples of Bangkok one is free to photograph. However, on entering the Temple of the Emerald Buddha, the visitor is explicitly invited to leave his camera — as well as his shoes — outside.

Time: Midmorning
Direction: Northwest
Lens: Wide angle

High temperature and humidity present a serious problem here. Most hotels are cooled by refrigeration — up to 40 degrees lower than exterior temperatures. When a camera is brought out of such an environment, moisture will condense on metal and lenses. It may take a short while for its temperature to rise to that of the outside area. When this is established, only then should one carefully remove the beads of moisture from his equipment and begin photography. The film supply for the trip should be kept cool and in dry places when possible. With hand luggage, it is quite possible to avoid any prolonged exposure of the film to heat.

Temple of the Dawn, Wat Arun / Bangkok, Thailand

ALTHOUGH THE GREAT POMP AND CEREMONY OF THE SIAMESE Kings is no more, Bangkok, the capital of the constitutional monarchy of Thailand, still has more flamboyant temples than any other city in the world.

Across the Menan Chao Phya (River Chao Phya) from the Temple of the Emerald Buddha is the Temple of the Dawn, Wat Arun. Its imposing central tower or *prang* is surrounded by four lesser *prangs,* one on each corner of the foundation. Basically made of brick, the exterior of the master *prang* is covered with mortar into which countless pieces of colorful glass, china and tile have been embedded, giving it a beaded splendor when seen from a distance.

Years ago this Buddhist monastery and temple was part of the Royal Palace compound. When the King's new *wat,* Phra Keo, was constructed on the opposite side of the river, Wat Arun and the Temple of the Dawn were eliminated from the royal unit. A *wat,* now loosely used to identify a single temple or building, was and still is a religious and social center of the Thais and is often surrounded by a wall. In a *wat* are various temples, chapels *(bots)* and often several *stupas*. Originally a *stupa* was created to hold and guard a relic of Buddha. Later, remains of kings and holy men have been added to *stupas*. The less elaborate *stupas* such as one sees in India are called Phra Chedi. The Temple of the Dawn of Wat Arun is a second type of *stupa* called Phra Prang, referring to its towers or *prangs*.

The *stupa* of the Temple of the Dawn quite logically has a distinct similarity to the Khmer temples of Angkor Wat in Cambodia since Thailand was a part of the Khmer empire for centuries.

The Temple of the Dawn stands majestically aloof from the myriads of Bangkok's temples, rising 240 feet into tropical skies on the right bank of the "mother of waters" — the Menan Chao Phya.

Time: Morning
Direction: West
Lens: Long

Bangkok's waterfront is quite interesting but very busy, and a high vantage point is recommended. Most merchants on the river's edge will allow a courteous photographer to use their river balcony — remove your shoes. Exposure is normal and if weather is fair it is simply a matter of a choice of foreground. A sunset silhouetting the temple prangs *is another picture.*

Entrance to the Chapel (Bot) of Wat Arun / Bangkok, Thailand

THAI ARCHITECTURE PREDOMINATES IN THIS GATEWAY IN contrast with the Khmer (Cambodian) style of the Phra Prang *stupa*, The Temple of Dawn already described. The brilliant green and orange tiles are typical of the Thai temple roofs. Along the edge of the eaves "the serpent shortens itself" while its head and tail project skyward at the end of the ridgepoles. The serpent which protected Gautama Buddha as he contemplated under the Bo tree is greatly revered. The tails of magic swans are also used as sky-tassels.

This approach to the *bot* or chapel is challenged by two gargantuan triple-faced ogres called "yaks." Grimacing and wielding the big stick, they undoubtedly will stop anyone with a guilty conscience.

These and other mythical figures as well as countless deities in the form of animals, humans and a mixture of the two in the Thai *wats* savor strongly of Hinduism mixed with Buddhism in this nominally Buddhist country.

Time: Midmorning
Direction: West
Lens: Normal or wide angle

The three major temples are all facing eastward and therefore are morning subjects. The two giant figures in this photograph are guarding a small shrine and are only a minor part of the great temple. This picture was made during the month of April prior to the monsoon period, yet close enough to take advantage of building thunder clouds. Tropical sunlight is nearly directly overhead from ten o'clock until two o'clock. With building clouds early morning light is nearly always best.

Klong Market / Bangkok, Thailand

THE CITY OF BANGKOK IS BISECTED BY THE GREAT WATER thoroughfare Menan Chao Phya, literally "mother of waters river." No matter how you spell it, and there are numerous ways to do so, it is always pronounced "chow-poo-yuh."

Many years ago the land on both sides of the river was honeycombed with canals — *klongs*. Gradually these canals on the east bank were filled in and today they are scarcely visible. A heavy traffic of automobiles, trucks, carts and motorcycles (pedicabs have been outlawed as too dangerous to passengers) rushes through the city of Bangkok where once "the free ones" moved on calm waterways.

On the west bank of the Chao Phya you are in the *klongs*, the canals, where life is conceived, lived and ended by the *klong* dwellers. These *klongs* interconnect and flow into the Chao Phya River. Traffic here is by small boats, poled or more often "chowed." Chowing is a process of steering and rowing a boat in unison by means of a swiveling oar secured in the stern. Then there are the peddlers who slowly paddle their boats overflowing with vegetables, fruits, food, cloth, notions or what-have-you past the front porches of the simple, almost primitive, homes of the *klong*-dwellers. The modern motor boat has not, unfortunately, been excluded.

A somewhat diminished romance of the *klongs* still exists. In the morning hours before ten o'clock you will find the vendors moving on the *klongs* at a slow pace lest they might overlook some tardy customer. Even a coffee break with snacks can be accomplished by the coffee-boat vendor. One almost expects to see the Fuller Brush man with his bag distributing free samples. Light-brown-skinned children in their nothings wade, brush teeth and play in the brown water of the *klongs* at their own front doorsteps.

As usual where people live on canals there is the matter of disposing of sewage and refuse. Theoretically the rising and lowering of the tide which comes up the river is a natural flushing system, but this plumbing arrangement is not always effective.

Some of the great teak logs grown in northern Thailand are floated down the Chao Phya and sidetracked into the sawmills built on the *klongs*. A teak tree at maturity may be over 100 years old and so saturated with water that it must be ringed and left standing a couple of years to die and dry before it can be floated downstream to Bangkok and the *klong* sawmills.

Time: Early morning
Direction: West
Lens: Wide angle

Canal life offers many picture possibilities. A high vantage point offers a good overall view. The friendly people are used to tourists' cameras and offer no objections. One could easily devote more photographs to such an area, all of which might surpass those of other areas of the world. It is with regret that many more of the photogenic subjects of this region cannot be given space here.

Shwe Dagon / Rangoon, Burma

THE UNION OF BURMA HAS TWO FAMOUS ROADS: KIPLING'S watery road, the Irrawaddy River, described with poetic imagery in his *Barrack Room Ballads* as "The Road to Mandalay"; and the Burma Road, that rugged 700-mile supply road over the mountains from Burma to China.

Equally renowned among travelers is the Shwe Dagon Stupa on the outskirts of Rangoon, Burma's largest city and seaport. A golden monument 168 feet above the city, created to hold several precious hairs from the head of Gautama Buddha, it is probably the most hallowed and impressive of all Buddhist shrines. Loosely called a pagoda, it is fundamentally a *stupa,* for only a *stupa* contains relics of the prophet. The *stupa* is a refinement of the ancient funeral mound of India — *a tope*. It is logical that Buddhists would seal their treasured objects related to their prophet in such a tomb. We could not resist a puckish speculation that under this gilded mass there might be buried one of those corkscrew curls so often seen covering the head of Buddha's image like a knobby skull cap. The golden spire of Shwe Dagon rises like a tapering funnel from the base mound containing the tonsured relics, and its crown is studded with native gems: rubies, emeralds, sapphires and diamonds. It is completely sheathed in leaves of beaten Burmese gold. Buddhists wishing to "gain merit" for themselves are often seen plastering additional squares of gold leaf on the shrine.

Surrounding the base of the *stupa* there is a proliferation of small shrines and pagodas. The ensemble reminded us of a huge maturing century plant encircled by its "chicks" — buds forever sprouting under its basal leaves.

Rangoon was a small fishing village when Shwe Dagon was first built and additions over a period of years have produced its present state of grandeur.

Time: Morning
Direction: West
Lens: Wide angle

A wide-angle lens is a must to capture the full height of this great stupa from within the temple grounds. The pavement here is very hot and one must remove his shoes. I advise early morning for this reason. There is no serious problem in this area with curious people. Protect film throughout all of Asia from heat and moisture.

Modern Hindu Temple / Delhi, India

THE MONOLITHIC PINK HINDU TEMPLE IN DELHI IS POPU-larly called the Birla Temple in honor of the Raja whose benevolence made it possible in 1938. This pantheon is dedicated to a miscellany of Hindu gods in any branch of Hinduism, Jainism or Sikhism. Buddha is also enshrined here.

Handsomely carved full-sized elephants and various other animals fill the adjoining courtyard, asserting their doctrine of reincarnation. Behind the temple a shaded garden with fountains and picnic areas under the trees for the pilgrims offers rest and contemplation. Beside one of the pools where the image of the sacred hooded serpent raises its stone head, we watched some low-caste Indian women wrapped in their *chuddars* splash sacred water on their children's faces.

* * * *

Since Hinduism controls the thinking and behavior of the majority of 500 million Indians, it is difficult for any visitor to understand the Indian way of life unless he has a small knowledge of Hinduism, the dominant religion.

Hinduism is prehistoric, as there is no solid date of its founder nor of the sacred writings, the Vedas. There has never been a more complicated religion in the history of the world. It it a bewildering multitude of deities, demons, spirits, symbols, myths and doctrines. Basically there is a trinity of gods: Brahma, the creator of the universe; Vishnu, the protector; Siva, the destroyer who destroys that there may be new life and who is also the god of reproduction. Brahma, a neuter, infinite and eternal, having finished his work of creation, is not worshiped as are Vishnu and Siva, considered males.

The doctrines of Hinduism are likewise bewildering to those who are not Hindus. Transmigration is fundamental. One's soul must pass at death into the body of another creature of lower or higher level, commensurate with the Hindu's earthly actions *(karma)* during his lifetime. Believing that man's soul may be reincarnated in any living creature, Hinduism forbids killing any form of animal life. Hence the overpopulation of cows, rats and all forms of animal life which increases human starvation in India. The caste system was born of Hinduism "to preserve pure descent" and castes still persist with a possible slight decrease in the upper strata.

In the sixth century B.C., a rich young Hindu, Gautama Buddha, became a reformer. His new cult of Buddhism denounced the caste system and promoted higher moral standards than those of Hinduism. Included in Buddhism, however, was the Hindu belief in reincarnation of the soul and no killing of any living creature. The ultimate goal of Buddhism was to reach *Nirvana,* a state of perfect bliss attained by the extinction of all self-desires. Buddhism in India was eclipsed and fused with the Hindu gods and mythology about 750 A.D. It does exist, however, in many variations in other Far Eastern countries today.

Two offshoots of Hinduism are Jainism and Sikhism which function today in India as does some Mohammedanism, since not all of the Muslims went to Pakistan at the time of the religious partition of India in 1947. Before that period, Islam was numerically the second religion of India. Presently, Christianity has 11 million adherents in India.

Time: Late morning
Direction: Northwest
Lens: Wide angle

Human activity around the temple is quite interesting. I was fortunate in being ready when a group of colorful women came by and appeared to be splashing water on themselves. I envied them in a way for it was over 114° F. that day in June. However, my driver informed me that they were splashing water on a bronze carving of a king cobra. They wouldn't repeat the ceremony so that I could make a second photograph.

Ghats / Banaras, India

To DRINK AND BATHE ONE'S BODY AT THE GHATS (STEPS) BOR-dering the sacred Ganges River at Banaras, then, at death, to be cremated here and have one's ashes tossed onto the filthy bosom of Mother Ganges is the apex of the soul's desire of the Hindu.

Driving from the airport to Banaras, we had received a macabre introduction to this Hindu custom. On the road we passed an oxcart carrying the sons of a dead man whose corpse wrapped in white cloth was strapped to the outside of the cart. Next, a deceased female in a bright orange shroud was approaching the Ganges carried on a frail litter. A trishaw pedaled in wobbly fashion was occupied only by a long white corpse bound across its seat.

A Hindu's great desire is to have sons who will escort his remains to the Ganges for cremation. The eldest son must remain until the corpse is consumed. Sometimes the family cannot afford enough firewood to complete the cremation, and a par-tially consumed body is pushed into the river where, floating, it may soon be pushed aside by pilgrims who are bathing very near the burning ghats.

The ghats stretch along the edge of the Ganges below ancient and crumbling palaces and homes. One spot is reserved for Moslems, another for Sikhs (easily distinguished by their long hair and full beards) and still another for the untouch-ables — sometimes called the scheduled class. Caste is not for-gotten even in purification rites. Over a thousand pilgrims come daily to purify themselves and gain merit for their next incarna-tion and are allowed by the government to stay three days in rest houses provided for them without charge.

Blind and leprous beggars border the entrance to the ghats with plaintive cries and outstretched hands. It is not a pretty picture.

Nor is Banaras a pretty city, but it *is* photogenic. Siva, the destroyer, is the favorite Hindu deity, and there are some 1500 dirty temples. In one of these, the Monkey Temple, a troop of scrofulous primates bounces about screeching and striking out at visitors. The traveler, having seen Banaras and the ghats, wishes to quickly depart. It is more pleasant to think of the Ganges where it is born high in the Himalayas in the clean snows than here at Banaras where humans seeking purity pollute it.

Time: Very early morning
Direction: Northward
Lens: Normal

Such photographs are made from small rowboats — steady enough for both still and movie cameras. Exposures should be fast enough to compensate for the boat's gliding movement. Courtesy here again — as everywhere — is a must, and one is asked to abstain from photographing the nearby burning ghats. The emotional tension here presents additional problems to the western visitor. Understanding and fortitude will help the photographer concentrate on his picture making.

Jain Temple / Calcutta, India

OUTSIDE OF A MYTH, LEGEND OR FAIRY TALE, WHOEVER heard of a jeweler building a temple studded with jewels in the land of the living? To add to this incredulity, he built it in Calcutta, India — that city of "black hole" infamy.

The Parasnath Jain Temple is diminutive and well incised like a precious jewel. Its minarets, domes and ogee arches are the basis for plaster surfaces on which brilliant mosaics — pieces of crystal and glass, precious and semiprecious stones — are partially imbedded. Depending on the time of day, this temple can appear to you as though it had been dipped in silver, gold or even in the rainbow itself.

Within the temple, the marble statue of a Jain Prophet wears a diamond in his forehead like a miner's lamp, while his revered feet rest on lotuses of silver. In front of the temple is a well-manicured formal garden with an assortment of small fanciful and realistic figures, dragons, mermaids, warriors, noblemen, nudes and even Chinese ornamental lamps. A pool reflects this aggregate creation of the Viceroy's Court Jeweler, a Jain devotee named Rai Buddree Das Bahadur Mookim who built the temple in 1867. Sheltered by a marble canopy, his own likeness in stone faces the entrance of the temple that the creator may not be forgotten. But it would be very difficult to forget this extraor-

dinary Jain Temple of Calcutta. It is even more difficult to believe it.

The Jain sect developed in India in 540 B.C., about 20 years earlier than Buddhism. Its founder Mahavira, an ascetic, emphasized austerity and abstinence to his followers so that they could control their bodily appetites. Jainism is similar to Hinduism and Buddhism in its belief in the transmigration of souls. There is no God in Jain tenets, only souls — a combination of consciousness and matter — which can reach a divine status. Even inorganic matter is believed to have dormant souls. One of the strictest observances of Jainism is to take *NO* life of any kind from a mosquito to an elephant, and they go to extremes to follow this stricture. Their 24 Jinas (saints) are worshiped, one of whom is enshrined in this glittering bijou, the Temple of Parasnath in Calcutta.

Time: Morning
Direction: North
Lens: Wide angle

India is an immensely photogenic country. Great temples, forts, and man-made edifices are in all areas of the country. Be tactful and sensitive to cultural differences in selecting your subject where people are concerned. Be prepared for sights unusual to the westerner and you will bring back photographs different than any others you will ever take.

THE RED, WHITE AND GREEN TRICOLOR OF INDEPENDENT INDIA floats above the Delhi gate of the Red Fort (Lal Qila), the red representing the Hindus, the green the Muslims, and the white the other religions of India. The most famous Mogul ruler of India, Shah Jahan, ordered the construction of the Red Fort in 1639 in order to move his capital from Agra to Delhi, the seventh Delhi to rise here. This was after the death of his Begum, Mumtaz Mahal. Shah Jahan's grandfather, Akbar, the founder of the Mogul dynasty of India, first brought Mohammedan architecture here — the architecture which is predominant in northern India.

Within these Islamic octagonal red walls with their domes and minarets still stand many impressive structures erected by Shah Jahan. One has only to walk through a gateway of this commanding walled city to imagine the exciting beauty, luxury, elegance and power which pulsed here only a little over three hundred years ago when Shah Jahan, his family and retainers dwelt here.

Inside the Marble Pavilion inlaid with gems and floored with rare Persian rugs stood the Peacock Throne. In this Audience Hall (Diwan-i-Khas) the Shah held his private chats and seminars. However, in his Public Audience Hall (Diwan-i-Am) built of red sandstone, he sat in state while elephants, caparisoned horses and hunting animals passed in elegant array before him. It was from here that this Solomon of Hindustan dispensed judgment publicly.

The Royal Baths, the Hammans, with hot and cold pools, offered a perfumed fountain as a final dash of scent to the bathers. Green glass windows filtered harsh Indian sunlight from this charming bathhouse.

Still another building quartered the Royal Band whose duty it was to play five times daily.

The Pearl Mosque of the Fort was built by Aurangzeb, the son who imprisoned his father Shah Jahan. As its name implies, it is a pearl both in size and beauty. Its domes, originally built of heavy copper and gilded, were destroyed and the present marble domes are much more suitable to the name, The Pearl Mosque.

In 1739, long after the death of Shah Jahan, the Persian invader Nadir Shah, taking advantage of a weak Mogul ruler of Delhi of that era, invaded Delhi, killing 20,000 Indians. Having sacked the city, he departed two months later ladened with his rich loot including the Peacock Throne, the Koh-i-nor diamond (mountain of light), plus all the private riches he could transport.

For visitors today there is a most realistic evening performance dramatizing the era of the Mogul Emperors, their lives, intrigues, loves and enemies. It is told in the spectacle within these walls called Son et Lumière. Even the sound of galloping horses and the heavy tread of elephants passing you is so realistic that you might be sitting in the Public Audience Hall with Shah Jahan watching this display of might and grandeur more than three hundred years ago.

Time: Late afternoon
Direction: East-northeast
Lens: Normal

Northern India is quite dry during winter and spring and until the last week of June when monsoons begin. I would advise visiting Delhi, Agra, and Banaras at least a month or two before the rains begin. Heat builds to over 110° daily during the month of June. Late August and September might be a more appropriate time to record the magnificent storm effects of the waning monsoon, as fluffy clouds and blue skies are characteristic of this time of year. One might be prepared to expect a few downpours of short duration, yet could be rewarded with a magnificent rainbow in the late afternoon. India is a real photographic challenge, offering constant opportunities to test one's photographic skill.

Taj Mahal / Agra, India

EVEN AS THE WHITE MARBLE OF THE TAJ REFLECTS THE gold of the sun in the daytime, it seems to absorb the silver light of the full moon giving it an ethereal quality of unworldliness. The bitter thoughts of Shah Jahan, who was imprisoned by his own son Aurangzeb for seven years in the Fort of Agra, must have occasionally been sweetened by the moments of memory of his wife and companion Mumtaz. Within his prison walls he could see the marmoreal beauty of the Taj where her body lay. This pinnacle of Mogul architecture, purely Persian in design, probably built of Indian marble from Rajputana, is inlaid with semiprecious stones of soft colors in the form of flowers and the decorative Arabic script of the Koran. It is carved with ultimate delicacy. No images of any kind are ever found in Moslem mosques or palaces.

When Shah Jahan ordered the building of the Taj, he also ordered the cessation of the building of Hindu temples. A whole city of men — 20,000 of them — builders and craftsmen, labored here for seventeen years to complete the Taj and the rare Mogul gardens surrounding it.

Following the founding of Islam (the Moslem religion) in 622 A.D., there has been a certain continuity in Islamic architecture with variations in different parts of the world. Throughout Christian countries there is no real similarity of architectural styles. The Islamic style of Persia with vaulted domes and minarets used in the building of the Taj, was brought into India by the Moguls and lasted throughout their dynasty.

Time: Late afternoon
Direction: North
Lens: Normal

For simulating night scenes, the technique used by the motion picture industry can be employed in still photography. Tungsten film is substituted for daylight film, giving a blue effect. A slight underexposure and a polaroid filter can be used. To make the scene appear realistic, care should be taken to use lighting that is relative to the moon's position. The moon, of course, must be double exposed onto the film later. Usually the night before full moon offers soft lighting before total darkness, requiring only a short wait for a second exposure. An exposure using only the moon's illumination is possible but requires a three-to-four minute exposure with fast film and lenses. The possibility of including moving people in the picture would be very poor.

Taj Mahal / Agra, India

THE STORY OF THE TAJ MAHAL IS THE SAGA OF A BELOVED woman whose husband gave her a marble halo when she died. Would that her memoirs had been written, for even though her life with the Shah was short — only eighteen years — no other woman has been so immortalized.

Born Arjumand Banu, Shah Jahan's wife was given the endearing name of Mumtaz Mahal, Elect of the Palace, when she became Begum. Two years younger than her husband, she married him in 1612. Shah Jahan did not assume the throne (after dethroning his father Jahangir) until 1627, so the palace life of Mumtaz as official consort of the reigning Shah was short — she died in 1630.

During the eighteen years of their marriage she bore the Shah fourteen children and still found time to be a wise companion and counselor to her husband, and to endear herself to the people of the realm by her charity and good works. When Mumtaz Mahal died, there was deep mourning for her. It is recounted that the Shah's handsome, neatly trimmed beard turned gray from the emotional shock. His grief culminated in two vows, one never to marry again, the other to build the world's most magnificent tomb for his beloved. He kept both vows.

Under the supervision of a master Persian builder the construction of the Taj began in 1631. When it was completed, the body of Mumtaz, which had been temporarily interred in the garden of the Taj, was placed under the marble dome in a tomb inlaid with semiprecious stones. The Mogul rulers were of the Islamic faith and Moslems bury their dead instead of burning them as do the Hindus.

The descriptions of the Taj are limitless. With some knowledge of the background of the woman who inspired it, we get an impression of this perfectly proportioned palace of death as something other than just a superb tomb. There is a certain purity to its color, delicacy in its tracery, and repose in its round domes and minarets. There is even a feminine touch — a mirror — in the long pool which reflects its beauty.

At the death of India's greatest Mogul ruler, Shah Jahan, his body was placed beside his beloved's under the great onion-shaped dome of the Taj. This type of architecture had not been seen in India prior to the days of the Mogul (Mongol) rulers, and the Taj was and still is the masterpiece of the Mogul dynasty.

Time: Afternoon
Direction: North
Lens: Normal

After three lengthy visits, I can only add my agreement that this is the world's most beautiful architectural masterpiece. It is photogenic from any angle and only weather and atmospheric conditions vary that additional aspect of its beauty. Those visiting the central part of India just prior to the late June monsoon season should keep in mind that heat convection currents can and usually do raise brown dust thousands of feet into the air, even on cloudless days. Late summer after the rains have fallen, winter, and spring offer better weather.

The Palace of the Winds / Jaipur, India

THE PINK CITY OF JAIPUR, IN THE STATE OF JAIPUR, WAS not built by the great Mogul builders but by the Rajput Maharaja Jai Singh II in 1728. Rajputana, a group of Indian states, was politically controlled by a strong, aggressive and aristocratic warrior caste of India, the Rajputs. The Mogul ruler Akbar recognized the power and ability of the Rajputs as did his son Jahangir. However, the last of the great Mogul rulers, Aurangzeb, was much less diplomatic in his relations with them — to his own discomfort.

Jaipur was designed by Rajput Singh II, the Maharaja whose scientific and astronomical skill were the basis of the modern design of the city which has thoroughfares over 100 feet wide intersected by narrow streets. This was unlike any other Indian city of that time. Many of the stucco buildings of Jaipur — not all by any means — are painted pink above the street level which is usually occupied by shops, merchants, markets and humans who are scarcely "in the pink."

The Palace of the Winds (Hawa Mahal), a blend of Mogul and Rajput architecture, is the most striking building in Jaipur. It was built seventy-one years after the city itself by the ruling Rajput Maharaja of that time. Much of its façade is pink sandstone. This nine-storied pyramidal wall of delicate artistry is a false front for the Maharaja's *zenana* or harem. Behind the pink screen was the *zenana* itself, a solid gray utilitarian building. From the well-vented peek holes his women — kept in *purdah* — could enjoy the street scenes of daily life, caravans of camels, horses, peddlers, traders, beggars and brilliant parades. Such fine amusement without the dreadful hazard of being seen! So many windows would imply a sizeable harem. Behind the Palace of the Winds, large cut stones on the ground, in geometric pattern and looking somewhat like a fantastic modern children's playground, are the astronomical observatory of the builder of Jaipur, Jai Singh II.

The last official Maharaja of Jaipur assumed his duties in 1949, and in 1967 was still governing with the advice of a ministry. A very modern young man, he was educated in England, with major interests in polo, car racing and flying. Yet this city does not reflect his modernity. You may see a native barber squatting on the sidewalk in the city square, his dull razor scraping the face of his customer who squats facing him.

As we attempted to escape from a crowd of children with fly-covered outstretched hands begging for anything we might have, we were stopped in our tracks by the sound of bagpipes. Oblivious to cows, trishaws and humans in his line of march, a brightly bedecked elephant, ridden by his *mahout,* lumbered down the main thoroughfare followed by a group of men dressed in their "Tuesday best." A scared young Hindu bridegroom on his way to his bride sat, with legs dangling, on the back of a horse whose bony form was partially hidden under a bright horse "sari." Behind him came the Indian band squeezing melancholy tones from — of all things — Scottish bagpipes. "Must be a big shot getting married to have the government band," remarked our Indian friend.

Time: Midmorning
Direction: West
Lens: Wide angle

The main obstacles to be avoided here are autos and people. There are several vantage points from which one can make his photograph over the heads of the curious. I would suggest careful preliminary view-finding prior to actual picture taking, particularly if a tripod is involved. I have had as many as two hundred people watching my preparatory work prior to exposing the film. An assistant can be most helpful. Exposure is by meter.

Meenakshi Gopuram / Madurai, India

MEENAKSHI (MEE NAK' SHEE), "THE FISH-EYED GODDESS," was the bride of the Hindu God Siva and although this Dravidian Hindu temple in Madurai is dedicated to her, the Sivalingam is the most revered area of the temple where the symbol of her husband Siva is worshiped. Only a Hindu may enter this inner sanctuary which is most holy to Hinduism.

Dravidian temples are unparallelled in their architectural form and are totally unlike any of those in northern India. The Dravidians of southern India are a dark-skinned Tamil-speaking merchant people who occupied India long before the Aryans invaded northern India and pushed the Dravidians southward.

The Aryans considered the Dravidians inferior to themselves socially, and many barriers arose between the north and south, some of which exist today. Dravidians, although Hindu by faith, do not subject themselves to the caste system of India.

In the city of Madurai, 280 miles by road south of Madras, is the incredible temple of Meenakshi. For over a century it was allowed to disintegrate. Then the entire temple was completely restored and its *gopuras* repainted in brilliant colors. Its nine gateways of varying sizes, called *gopuras,* penetrate the four walls which surround the temple compound. (The view here is of the east *gopuram*.) Each *gopuram* is so lavishly decorated with figures of deities, lesser gods, monsters, animals and human abnormalities that there is scarcely a breathing space between them. The figures are cast in stucco and applied to the outside of the brick *gopuram*.

Diminishing in size as it tapers upward, the *gopuram* is crowned with an elongated dome. Anchored in the dome are Sivaistic symbols and large brass vessels looking like finials.

During the great celebration in 1960 at the completion of the restoration of the temple, Hindu priests standing on top of the renovated *gopuras* poured holy water over these brilliant-colored structures while camphor fires flared dramatically from the top to the sound of horns, drums and bells. Fortunately, time has mellowed those garish hues which covered this frenzied pantheon.

Around the Golden Lily Pond in the midst of the temple are roofed halls (*mandapams*) surfeited with enormous carved stone figures of hundreds of deities, some with multiple arms and legs, and most of them in dancing positions proudly displaying bulbous breasts and distended bellies. Even many of the stone pillars in the Hall of a Thousand Pillars are carved with large-hipped deities and figures half-man and half-animal. Whoever were the unsung sculptors, they did not indulge in delicacy of art or thought. Good art was overpowered by their devotion to the supernatural. Perhaps the most interesting bit of sculpture seen through the gloom of these *mandapams* or halls is the trio of figures in which Vishnu is puckishly presenting Meenakshi to her bridegroom Siva, the *raison d'etre* for this particular Temple of Meenakshi, which no traveler in India should miss visiting.

Time: Morning
Direction: Southwest
Lens: Wide angle

Extreme heat, though less humidity than in Bangkok, presents its usual problems, yet subject matter is overwhelming, making this side trip from Madras well worth the effort. Only in this southern part of India can one find this style of architecture. Photography within the temple bathing area — a rectangular pool of sacred water with steps leading down to it on all four sides — is limited to the hours from one to four P.M. Other areas within the great walls are unrestricted.

A TRAVELER HEADING FOR KASHMIR OFTEN HAS A STARRY-eyed look as though he were entering the vestibule of the Pearly Gates. During the British rule of India, in India's stifling summer heat the English residents sought the cool retreat of a houseboat on the spring-fed Dal Lake at Srinagar, Kashmir's summer capital. World War II brought a cessation of holidays. Srinagar, without tourist income and lacking winter fuel, broke up many of its older houseboats for firewood. Today visitors have returned in flocks and some new houseboats are being built each year. But the snow-covered Pir Punjal Mountains in the distance are changeless.

Waterway vendors in their *shikaras* (Kashmir gondolas) filled with heterogenous merchandise from toothpaste to fox skins, ply the canal of the lake where the deodar houseboats are anchored to the shore. They are watching for the first sign of morning activity before they timidly knock at your front door. It is hard to resist these soulful-eyed, persistent, silver-tongued salesmen. "Ah, memsahib, you do not remember me! Now I have a beard. Since you were here I have been to Mecca and I am now a Haji. I have come again to show you my beautiful fabrics." I remembered him only too well. A joyous-spirited Moslem wearing his jaunty karakul cap who came every morning with a large smile and a high singsong "Goodmorning, goodmorning," was our favorite.

There are many fine craft items in Kashmir which are brought to the doorstep of your houseboat by the *shikara* merchants: brass, silver, jewelry, leather, fabrics, woodwork, countless articles made of papier mâché and the famous Kashmir shawls made from the under-fleece of the Kashmir goat. This wool is called *pashm*.

One no longer expects to find the historical *Shahtoush* shawl made from the finest under-chin hair of the Himalayan Kashmir goat. The former Maharaja of Kashmir each year until 1947 sent a *shahtoush* shawl to the British Crown. As fine as spun spider silk and soft as down, these natural wool, tan colored shawls are worth a "pretty penny" today. Kashmiris take pride, and rightfully so, in their exquisite oriental hand-loomed rugs. To see them you must go to the shops in Srinagar where they are sold, or to the dark factories in the old town where families of men and boys sit at their upright looms for days and years swiftly knotting by hand the intricate patterns of these rare rugs. Many Persian patterns have been copied and they have developed their own patterns also. We met expert rug merchants here from Europe and Australia who claimed that some of the finest oriental rugs are loomed in Kashmir.

Swiftly paddled *shikaras* carrying vegetables to town from the farming islands pass the houseboats each morning laden with tomatoes, cucumbers and mounds of kohlrabi — cabbage turnips. From the volume produced, one assumes that kohlrabi must be a favorite vegetable of the Kashmiris whose staple diet is rice. After a morning of self-restraint among these importunate water merchants, when a quiet little man arrives in his *shikara* holding up to your view a small black box labelled in large white letters, "Hairdresser — Expert Massage" you are tempted to succumb. All this is part of the fun of life on a houseboat.

Time: Early morning
Direction: Westward
Lens: Normal

Though beautiful scenery surrounds Srinagar, the most unusual sights are the colorful houseboats on Lake Dal, and the small shikaras *filled with merchandise. If you buy flowers one morning there will be two beautiful boats awaiting your rising the next morning. It is a photogenic area full of good feeling for the vendors who can't take "no" as a final word but will continue their offerings as long as you grant them audience. Exposure should be a bit greater than meter reading of dark water.*

Waterway Houses / Srinagar, Kashmir

OF THE THREE AND ONE-HALF MILLION KASHMIRI PEOPLE, 75 percent are Moslems and the majority of them are farmers. Approaching Srinagar by air in the summertime, flying over the green Vale of Kashmir 5000 feet above sea level, you see the many irrigated rice paddies and corn fields covering the floor of the valley which is encircled by snow-covered mountains. But the intimate life of the vegetable "truck" farmer is centered on the so-called floating islands of Dal Lake. Most of these islands have taken root in the shallow lake and are not apt to wander away from home.

One of the greatest joys of the houseboat visitor is to be comfortably *shikaraed,* while sitting on spring cushions and shaded by a frilled canopy, through the waterways which meander between the islands. With his heart-shaped paddle, often his *hookah* (his hubbly-bubbly water pipe) and a small charcoal stove (or in winter his small pottery heater, the *kangri,* filled with hot ashes), he seems as content as you are to spend hours pushing your *shikara,* "The Abode of Love," through weedy canals or down open waterways.

The island farm houses, three- or four-storied thatched-roofed houses made of brick and wood and often with balconies, serve a multiple purpose. The upper story just under the roof is usually open to the weather and is a storage area for everything. The second and third stories are living quarters, and here the eldest son usually brings his bride to live with his family. The lower areas accommodate their small animals — ducks, chickens, dogs, cats, goats and sometimes a cow. Flocks of ducks and their downy ducklings may wander far from home but always return at night.

There are occasional shops along the canals with bright fabrics or housewares for the farmers' wives. Playing along the banks, joyous children, whose language is Kashmiri, communicate with you by their smiles and handwaving as they shout "tee tee Madame, tee tee Madame!" The salutation seems to refer to male or female. The island gardens, right at the front doorstep, must be cultivated, irrigated and fertilized by hand to produce onions, tomatoes, cucumbers, eggplants, squashes and the inevitable kohlrabi for the markets at Srinagar. A woman empties small baskets of lake-bottom soil in neat piles around the edge of her cucumber garden. It looks like a border of big black thimbles. Men in shallow boats are seen daily pushing to the bottom of the lake long poles which they twist round and round, wrapping weeds upon them — like twisting taffy. Piled high on their boats, these weeds will serve both as fertilizer and fodder for their animals. In the early winter months, long after the pink lotus blossoms have finished blooming, you will see men pulling up the long subterranean stalks of the lotus to be used for fodder also. Were it not for this constant human dredging the lake would be clogged with vegetation.

There is a tranquility here in the farm islands not found in the dirty streets of Srinagar where bicycles, two-wheeled, horse-drawn tongas, and automobiles thread their way through the heavy foot traffic of an ancient city.

Time: Late morning
Direction: Southwest
Lens: Normal

These weathered four-hundred-year-old wooden homes offer bleak architecture, highlighted with colorful silk hung from small shops along the canals. Exposure is rather difficult to read by meter due to the extreme contrast range, though reading of wood in sunlight will give a good basic exposure.

Dal Lake / Srinagar, Kashmir

THERE IS A SOFT VELVETY TEXTURE TO THIS PHOTOGRAPH — twilight peace over Lake Dal. If we had stretched out a hand to touch it, it might have vanished.

In the cool of the early evening, when we were there, a few Kashmiri women were gathering vegetation for fodder from the lake bottom with their long poles. Sitting far out on the pointed bows of their shallow boats, huddled under their *phirans* (baggy-sleeved coats) or wrapped in their *chuddars* (shawls), they simulated figureheads on bowsprits.

The handsome palace of the Hindu Maharaja who formerly ruled this predominantly Moslem state of over three and one-half million people overlooks the lake near here. It is now a hotel. At this end of the lake the Moguls built their pleasure gardens — Nishat, Shalimar, Naseem and Chasma Shahi — filled with flowers, terraced waterfalls, fountains and great shade trees, chenars (sycamores) and evergreens. The gardens have been well preserved and in the summer crowds of orientals and occidentals throng these gardens on holidays. These parks are peppered with khaki-uniformed police and soldiers which India keeps in Kashmir in large numbers, much to the distaste of the Kashmiri.

The smallest of these pleasure gardens — Chasma Shahi — impresses the visitor as an intimate sanctuary rather than a public garden. A crystal spring rises in the garden. It was this Royal Spring which intrigued Shah Jahan and inspired him to create this oasis. The spring descends from the garden and enters Dal Lake, 5000 feet above sea level in the Vale of Kashmir.

Time: Late evening
Direction: South
Lens: Long

Cooperation from models helps, as late evening light is rather weak and exposure is quite critical. The meter reading drops fast as the sun nears the horizon. Often a simple scene such as this can be quite rewarding. I suggest bracketing exposures since film is the least costly item in travel photography. Incidentally, it is always advisable to obtain permission when photographing people anywhere. Women in some countries are often quite reluctant, yet a bit of friendly persuasion is almost always effective.

Swayambhunath Stupa / Kathmandu, Nepal

LEGENDS AND FANTASIES ARE INCOMPATIBLE WITH OUR human experience, and yet when a legend is exploded and the logical answer is found, we often feel a bit bankrupt. Nepal's great legend has been that of the Abominable Snowman, the Yeti, the evil monster who, with his feet pointing backwards, stalked the Himalayas leaving only his great footprints. In 1962 an expedition of explorers and mountain climbers debunked this myth, concluding that the Yeti is the rare Tibetan Blue Bear.

The small country of Nepal — 100 miles by 500 miles — has been almost as legendary as the Yeti and as inaccessible as Mount Everest, "the Goddess mother of the world." Although the Kingdom of Nepal has never been under foreign domination, it was rigidly controlled for one hundred years by the Rana family of the Prime Minister who dethroned the Nepalese King in 1850 and took over the reins of government. The Ranas kept the gates of Nepal closed to the world, not wishing their dictatorship challenged. Pressure from India and China finally caused the fall of the Rana dynasty and the King was restored in 1950.

Hinduism and Buddhism are again found entwined here. The King is considered the reincarnation of the Hindu God Vishnu. On a hill in Patna, overlooking Kathmandu, Nepal's capital, the Buddhist temple of Swayambhunath has existed since 250 B.C. This true *stupa*, whose square tower displays four pairs of all-seeing eyes, rises above a courtyard where hundreds of sheltered images of Buddha receive the worshiper's offering of rice and bits of food placed in their immobile laps. Dogs and monkeys who overrun the temple yard have no scruples about leaping into these food pockets and devouring the offerings. Rows of prayer wheels, small cylinders on spindles filled with tightly compacted sheets of prayers, are rotated by passing worshipers to speed their supplications to their deities.

Kathmandu lies in a valley in the midlands of Nepal, 4500 feet above sea level, and is seldom touched by snow. Between the world's highest mountain range in the north and the fetid jungle of the Terai in the south, Kathmandu in the valley of Nepal has an equable climate. Over high Himalayan foot trails hundreds of Tibetans have found their way to a refuge in Nepal in recent years. A roadless country for many years, it now has about 500 miles of roads, one of which connects Nepal with India. Of the many races in Nepal, the Newars (original inhabitants), the Gurkhas and the Sherpas are the names most familiar to us.

Kathmandu was formerly Kantipur. Still another "once upon a time" relates that the Tree of Paradise appeared at a parade disguised as a man. Recognized, he was held captive until he promised to provide his captor with a single tree large enough to build an entire house. His ransom was a huge sal tree. The wooden house which its lumber built is still standing in Kathmandu — so it is said. *Kath* = wood. *Mando* = house. Thus Kantipur became Kathmandu.

Time: Late afternoon
Direction: Eastward
Lens: Wide angle

The Buddhist temples of Kathmandu seemed to be more confined by the surrounding buildings than in other cities, requiring the use of a wide-angle lens. Here variable weather often determines the time of day one can photograph his subject. Throughout Asia a car and driver are very helpful. Not that protection is needed, but often assurance is needed, for information about unusual customs, to obtain permissions, and so forth.

Mt. Demavend / Tehran, Iran

A LONG THE NORTHERN BORDER OF IRAN AND AT THE SOUTH end of the Caspian Sea, the Elburz Mountains rise to peaks of 11,000 and 13,000 feet. Mount Demavend, northeast of Tehran, soars to 18,600 feet, surpassing by 3000 feet the famous white tower of France, Mt. Blanc. Myths and legends are often attached to high places in the world, and there are several extant about Mt. Demavend.

Zoroasterism was Persia's religion before Persia was subjugated by Islam. One legend says that their prophet Zoroaster took on the form of a huge and wise bird and lived on the slopes where he could oversee his people. Another, that an offending tyrant was shackled in a cave near the top of this dormant volcano and still breathes out sulphurous vapors of his wrath through its craters. A more credentialed historical note indicates that a great Assyrian king who conquered Damascus also turned his armies in the direction of northern Iran and celebrated victory on the mountain called Demavend.

Iran, peaceful today under Shah Mohammed Riza Pahlevi, is the home of nomads who have pitched their black goatshair tents at the base of Mt. Demavend where they find pasturage for their flocks.

The Harhaz River rises near Mt. Demavend and flows north into the Caspian Sea as do many other short rivers rising in the Elburz Mountains. Into these cold rivers many roe-filled sturgeon go to spawn if they have escaped the nets of the Iranian caviar fishermen in the salty Caspian, 90 feet below sea level.

Time: Late afternoon
Direction: North
Lens: Normal

I had planned representing this area with a photograph of the Peacock Throne which is one of this part of the world's great attractions, but was greatly disappointed to find this closed to visitors due to a remodeling prior to the coronation of the Shah. However, to my surprise I was able to photograph Mt. Demavend en route to the Caspian Sea. A late April snowstorm had hidden Japan's Fuji from my camera a third time, yet here, comparable in beauty and half again as high, is this majestic 19,000-foot volcano of the Middle East, only an hour's drive east of Tehran — a real bonus to this area's visitor.

Shah's Mosque / Isfahan, Iran

IN ISFAHAN, THE NAME OF THE FAMOUS PERSIAN MONARCH Shah Abbas is so constantly on the lips of Iranians that automatically it has become "Shabis." Shah Abbas as a child was puppet ruler of Persia but during his lifetime he welded many races into a great nation. While Good Queen Bess was ruling during the golden age of England, Shah Abbas established Isfahan as his capital in 1592 and built his own matchless royal mosque, Masjid-i-Shah, at one end of the large rectangular polo field which was the median of his new city, called Maidan-i-Shah.

His relatively small five-storied palace, Ali Kapu — no elevators — gave him a vantage point from which to oversee this original sport of Persia, polo. As many as 150 horsemen on each team kept the action exciting. This Maidan also served as a parade ground and a meeting place for the crowds. Remodeled in recent years, it has become a public park with flower gardens and a reflecting pool.

Fortunately for the traveler, the mosques, palaces, schools and other buildings of Isfahan built by Shah Abbas have been well preserved as masterpieces of the perfection of Islamic architecture. They are not used by the Muslims for worship today, but it is not uncommon to see a Muslim unroll his prayer rug before the *mihrab* — the prayer niche — of the mosque and put himself in the attitude of prayer in Masjid-i-Shah.

There is a pleasing rapport between the many shades of blue, and other colors used in the polychrome tiles of the bulbous domes, delicate tapered minarets and exteriors as well as interiors of the mosques in Isfahan.

Here in the Shah's own mosque, so that the *mihrab* would be in perfect alignment with the Holy City of Mecca in Arabia, it was necessary to build the body of the mosque at an acute angle to the entrance which faces directly onto the street at the end of the Maidan.

Time: Afternoon
Direction: Southward
Lens: Normal

All mosques are positioned relative to Mecca, and, depending upon their position east, west, north or south of this holy place, are oriented differently. Here the front entrance faces due north while the inner entrance faces northeast so that those kneeling in prayer face Mecca to the southwest. Midday light is quite poor; evening or morning light is much better, particularly in late spring and summer. This modern city of the Middle East was a real surprise and a highlight of an Asian visit.

Shah's Mosque at Night / Isfahan, Iran

UNFORTUNATELY SHAH ABBIS NEVER HAD THE OPPORTUNITY to see his rare mosque at night under the artificial light of today's heavy wattage. The myriad-colored stalactite decoration beneath the perfectly proportioned arch shimmers under artificial light like an opalescent honeycomb.

In 1935, under the rule of Riza Shah Pahlevi, the first Pahlevi of the line and the man who took over the Persian government by a *coup d'etat,* the name Persia was changed to Iran. The reasons for this are somewhat obscure but apparently it was done to create an awareness of the early Aryan stock of Persia which came from Asia and other northern countries. However, it is the opinion of some anthropologists that the southern province of Parsa (Fars) "contains the oldest remains of man in Iranian soil." Persian is the spoken language of the country, but it is written in Arabic. There is a great mixture of races in Iran today: Arabs, Turks, Mongols, Armenians, as well as many powerful nomadic tribes, these latter having their own dialects and customs.

Isfahan, "the most beautiful city in the world," was Persia's capital for many years. The Peacock Throne, India's treasure that Nadir Shah brought to Persia in 1739 as a spoil of war, was in Isfahan for some years. However, the capital was transferred to Tehran in 1788 and with it went the throne, a large box-like platform. On this famous — or infamous — piece of furniture in Tehran, Mohammed Riza Shah was officially crowned in October, 1967. He is the second of the Pahlevi dynasty, having succeeded his father who abdicated in 1941. The son had been a benevolent ruler of Iran for twenty-six years before he placed the jeweled crowns on his own head and that of his young queen — making them King of Kings and Empress of Iran, respectively — amidst great fanfare and ceremony. They have a handsome young brown-eyed son who it is anticipated in due process of time will succeed to the throne and carry on the Pahlevi dynasty.

Time: Sundown through total darkness
Direction: South
Lens: Normal

A number of interesting places are lit after dark and offer unusual possibilities for the photographer. At this location the sun set at 6:30 P.M. when I was there, and the lights did not come on until 8:00, leaving a long waiting period. Quite a crowd gathered around the camera on a tripod while we were waiting for the second exposure. The Iranians were very friendly and courteous. University students were full of questions about America and helped pass away the time interestingly. The second exposure was by meter reading and under these circumstances only one exposure is correct.

Persepolis / Shiraz, Iran

PERSE POLIS = PERSIAN CITY. IT IS ONLY 40 MILES FROM Shiraz. The name originated in Parsa or Persis in southern Iran centuries ago. When Islam overran Persia, many of the Parsis fled to India with their Zoroastrian faith where they are even today known as Parsees. But Persepolis still stands in grandeur in southwest Persia with the invisible word "history" written across its name.

Scholars of recent years studying the cuneiform tablets unearthed at Persepolis believe this massive limestone edifice was not the working or political capital of Persia, but a special palace built by Darius I for use particularly at great celebrations of national importance. Cyrus the Great, founder of the far-flung Persian Empire and remembered for his liberation of the captive Jews, picked the site for Persepolis but died in 529 B.C. before its construction was started by Darius I. Unlike Babylon, built of bricks which disintegrated into a rubble heap, Persepolis was fashioned of stone of such superior quality — hewn from the great cliff which is the city's backdrop — that even the wrath of its final conqueror, Alexander the Great, could not completely destroy it.

At this ceremonial palace for festivals, the Persian deity, Ahura Mazda (God of Light), envisioned by the prophet Zoroaster, was besought to give aid and protection to the Persians. Zoroasterism is based on man's struggle between good and evil. Zoroaster's principles were "Think good, speak good, do good," expressed in the positive in contrast with the Shinto shrine in Nikko, Japan, where the three monkeys are demonstrating "hear no evil, speak no evil, see no evil."

Darius, the builder of Persepolis, was a powerful monarch and organized the empire into provinces (satrapies) for better government and for supervised collection of taxes which he imposed. But he overextended his ability when he invaded Greece and was soundly defeated at Marathon in 490 B.C. Undismayed by this failure, he was planning another attack on Greece when he died, leaving his son Xerxes to avenge his death. Xerxes, hiring the most capable Phoenician seamen of the time to man his fleet in the Aegean Sea, seized and burned Athens. But he was outwitted by the furious Greeks at Salamis in 480 B.C. and again defeated.

Xerxes completed the great palace complex at Persepolis. The tall pillars seen standing on the high stone platform were part of his Audience Hall which was roofed with timbers from Cedars of Lebanon. In this *Apadana* his own people as well as the great of the world came to his feet bringing gifts and revenues. The life-sized bas reliefs on the stone walls of the great staircases of Persepolis which remain, reveal the fine workmanship of their sculptors. Prevalent in these figures is the hooked nose which was considered a feature of great beauty by the Persians.

These ruins of Persepolis which we see today are a monograph of the fierce destruction wrought by the Greek Conqueror Alexander the Great who burned and looted Persepolis in retaliation for the Persians' destruction of Athens. An eye for an eye! Retribution had been served! The Persian Empire, as such, shortly went into decline.

Time: Late afternoon
Direction: Eastward
Lens: Normal

This is somewhat of a photographic challenge. Its history and importance are outstanding, but subject matter is lacking, particularly when atmospheric conditions are not complimentary. Approximately a dozen columns remain standing and many of the stone images and carvings are well preserved though faces often have been destroyed. Crosslighting is helpful in making the reliefs discernible. Late evening light warms the color of the buff stone. The guards will gladly wait a short while if you care to catch the last rays of the setting sun.

Waterwheels (Norias) / Hama, Syria

NO WISE MAN BUILDS HIS HOUSE UNLESS WATER IS AVAILable. No city ever endures without a source of water nearby. Deserted cliff dwellings of the Indians of the southwestern United States are dramatic evidence of the disappearance of water.

Some of the great Persian waterwheels built on the Orontes River near the ancient city of Hama in southwest Syria—thought by some to be older than Damascus — still rotate and lift water from the flowing Orontes River into the stone aqueduct which leads to the irrigation ditches of the farms of Hama at a higher level than the river. Today there are only nine of these great *norias* — undershot waterwheels — functioning whereas in the fourteenth century thirty of them in sundry sizes existed. The largest was 80 feet in diameter. The steadily moving water of the river fills the small buckets attached to the wheel. The wheel rotates upward pushed by the force of the water, dumps the water into the aqueduct and descends both by gravity and the force of the water. This is called an undershot waterwheel.

Nearby is the picturesque city of Hama built between the deep banks of the Orontes River. It was the creation of the Hittites and was an important center of commerce and communications. Bible history tells us in Chronicles II that Israel's King "Solomon went to Hamath-zobah and prevailed against it." The list of prevailers is a long one: Assyrians, Persians, Greeks, Romans, Arabs, Crusaders and Turks. Even under the Ottoman Turks (Muslims), Christianity was not banned from Hama and still exists there. The Turks held Syria until after World War I at which time it was mandated to France. It received its independence after World War II, in 1946.

Hama's many conquerors, aware of the vital ingredient of life — water — did not destroy these famous waterwheels which "ground out the song of the river." In spite of modern turbines, the faithful weary old waterwheels of Hama still function but their senile voices now groan with the infirmities of old age.

Time: Afternoon
Direction: Northwest
Lens: Normal

Occasionally a photographer will go hundreds or thousands of miles off the beaten tourist road to photograph something relatively unimportant in the world's places of beauty or known interest. I had long wanted to photograph the norias *of Hama. It was disappointing that I was unable to remain in Hama overnight for an early morning picture of these creaking monsters. I would like to have seen the golden light of sunrise striking the weathered wood of these ancient wheels. But I was very fortunate in getting any picture for war was imminent and only two days later, June 5, 1967, the Arab-Israeli War began. Of even greater disappointment was the cancellation of my trip to Petra in Jordan.*

IN THE SPRING OF THE YEAR IT IS A PLEASANT EXPERIENCE TO drive inland from the coastal city of Beirut, Lebanon, up the wedge-shaped valley of Bekka. The Lebanon Mountains to the east are blended patches of farms and green terraces. Apple, cherry and fig trees, red poppies and wild roses flourish. Arabs with their flocks of long-haired sheep and goats have pitched their black tents on the valley floor. Looking west you see the Anti-Lebanon Mountains, but the famous Cedars of Lebanon are not visible. Only a few hidden groves of those famous giants have escaped the canker of man's destruction.

From this vibrant living earthy atmosphere, you reach the apex of the pie-wedge valley and come suddenly upon the impressive and necrophilic remains of ancient Baalbek. The name "Baal" — the plural of which is Baalim — is a semitic word meaning "possessor." Baal was not the specific name of any one deity but a comprehensive name which might cover one or more gods having local names in various communities. Knowing this, we are able to understand how this temple retained its name from the time of the Caananites who established it (preceding the time of the Israelites) through its occupation by many nations which set up their own system of gods and still called it The Temple of Baal. Limestone used in the building of Baalbek was quarried nearby and is still marked by a gigantic square granite shaft never removed from its bed.

The Romans possessed Baalbek at the time of Christ, both the temple and the city adjoining it. Their Baalim was a trinity of deities, Jupiter, Venus and Mercury, to whom the Romans built imposing temples, remnants of which are extant. The six Corinthian limestone pillars, 62 feet high and 7 feet in diameter,

which remain standing as part of the Temple of Jupiter — monoliths against a blue sky — re-create the feeling of the early grandeur of Baalbek.

The Greeks, preceding the Romans, had called it Heliopolis since they worshiped the Sun God. Under the Roman Emperor Constantine, a Christian church was built within the walls of Baalbek. In 635 A.D. the Arabs, whose Islamic faith tolerated no images or idols, converted the Temple of Baal into a fortress. These great stone masterpieces of man were toppled by a series of earthquakes which left Baalbek a rubble heap. Between 1898 and 1905 a group of German archaeologists reconstructed much of what you see at Baalbek today. This work was followed by French restoration in 1932 and now the Lebanese are continuing it. To date the most convincing restoration has been done in the Temple of Bacchus.

As you climb through the ruins of Baalbek you are aware that you are treading on the skeleton of a once-mighty temple whose great stone ribs lie broken at your feet and whose flesh — the great carvings of this temple — has not entirely decayed.

Time: Morning
Direction: Northwest
Lens: Wide angle

I've never been too impressed with Roman ruins from a photographic viewpoint unless the scene is accompanied by dramatic clouds, a storm or late evening light. But I was impressed with the immensity of Baalbek and, compared with the Roman Forum, it must surely have surpassed it in grandeur. At the time I was there workmen were stringing lights among the ruins for a festival of plays, operas and the like that are normally performed every summer and which draw thousands of visitors. I assume that these were cancelled due to the war which broke out immediately after my visit. It seems safe to assume that in more peaceful years these festival events will again take place.

Mount of Olives / Jerusalem

IT IS DIFFICULT TO PUT YOUR FOOT ON ONE INCH OF GROUND on the Mount of Olives which does not have religious, historical or emotional significance to Christians, Jews and Moslems. Neither spectacular in height nor beauty, it is so closely related to the many poignant experiences of Jesus and his disciples that it is still deeply cherished more than 1900 years after he ascended from the top of the Mount.

The green olive trees under which Christ prayed are gone, probably cut by the Romans about 70 A.D. The present trees, over a thousand years old, have tired arthritic trunks and a minimum of leaves, but give credence to the earlier olive grove here called Gethsemane, meaning olive press. Doubtless there was a stone olive-oil press nearby. It it reasonable to surmise that Jesus followed one of the paths leading over the Mount of Olives to Bethany on the eastern slopes — a shortcut to the home of his warm friends Mary, Martha and Lazarus.

In the garden of Gethsemane Jesus prayed in agony, here he met his disciples the night before his crucifixion by the Romans, and here he was betrayed by his disciple Judas Iscariot. This garden, so sacred to Christian belief, has been walled and tended by Franciscan Monks since 1861. And here also is the Church of All Nations.

Above the garden on the hillside, somewhat hidden by the surrounding trees, you see the blue-gray onion domes of the Russian Orthodox Church of St. Mary Magdalene built by Czar Alexander III in memory of his mother. It seems fitting that Mary Magdalene who traveled with Jesus on his final journey to Jerusalem, witnessed his crucifixion and his burial, who returned with spices to anoint his body and found the empty tomb, should be remembered here, but few visitors to the Mount of Olives even know the name of this little church on the hillside.

For years fortunate Jews have been interred in a traditional burying ground on the slopes of the Mount awaiting the resurrection day of the Great Judgment here. Moslems are buried across the River Kidron at the foot of the Mount of Olives, and believe that those who cannot walk a hairline with the help of their Prophet Mohammed at the Great Day of Judgment will be doomed eternally.

There is a group of small buildings on the top of the mountain and recently a large modern hotel has been constructed by the Jordanians for tourists — a sad commercial corona for Olivet to those who are purists.

Time: Afternoon
Direction: Eastward
Lens: Normal

This is an area of great importance to many of the people of the world, yet photogenically it's a difficult area to photograph. Many of the Biblical places of Christ's time have been covered by later structures. However, the Mount of Olives remains much the same. Afternoon light is preferable, but from the Mount of Olives one could look westward and photograph the sun's first rays of morning light striking the dome of the rock in Jerusalem.

OF THE SEVEN WONDERS OF THE WORLD, THE ANCIENTS listed the Pyramid of Cheops at Giza on the outskirts of Cairo as the Number One Wonder of the World, both in magnitude and permanence. This enormous tomb was built for the Egyptian King Khufu (Cheops), founder of the Fourth Dynasty. His origin is scarcely known, his date of reign is disputed (either 3969 or 2900 B.C.) and his death was heralded with rejoicing by his subjects. However, after milleniums, his tomb exists almost intact, while other great monuments of lesser age have crumbled or been destroyed.

As is true of all peoples of the world, the Egyptians' behavior was controlled by their religious beliefs. Believing that each human had five souls and that the soul would return to the body sometime after death, the Egyptians' great purpose in life was to prepare for this eventuality. Thus, mummification of the body and the building of tombs impenetrable by grave robbers became an obsession. Grave robbers, however, were more successful than the supposed impenetrability of stone sarcophagi!

Khufu (Cheops) closed the Egyptian temples and impressed thousands of luxury-living priests and attendants into his 300,-000-man work corps to build his pyramid. For this labor they received their food and clothing. The Greek "father of history" Herodotus recounts that hieroglyphics at the base of Cheops' tomb recorded that for radishes, onions and garlic for the workers two million dollars were expended. One wonders if these were mere tidbits added to their diet.

How, how, how were they built? This is the first question which besets you when you look upon the Pyramids of Giza. Thirteen acres of stones solidly piled in pyramidal form and surfaced with polished limestone contained hidden passages and secreted burial chambers. Quarried stone brought on barges from 700 miles up the Nile River was sledged on rollers up a great stone causeway to Giza. How these mammoth rough-hewn stones were pyramided to 150 feet in height is still partially conjecture. Sand ramps to move them up on inclined planes is one theory. Herodotus believed that they were lifted by "machines," planks used as levers which were used and reused. The Egyptians left no description, and 3000 years passed after the Pyramid of Cheops was built before there was any written description of it.

With the hatred Cheops incurred, it is doubtful that the enslaved Egyptians ever gave him the honor of burial in his despised tomb. Undoubtedly they had no desire for his *bai* (soul) to return to his *ka* (body) at any time. Grave robbers may have given them this satisfaction for his mummified body has never been found. The two lesser pyramids beside the tomb of Khufu were built for his successor, Kafra, whose image is in replica in the face of the Sphinx, and the third tomb was that of his son Menkaura.

In 642 A.D., with the arrival of the Islamic Arab conquerors who were violently intolerant of all religions save Mohammedanism, there was no compunction about removing the polished casing of stones of these pyramids to build their own mosques as they began the erection of the city of Cairo. An earthquake in 1301 stripped the remaining covering from the pyramids, but nothing as yet has removed the First Wonder of the World from its moorings.

Time: Late afternoon
Direction: Northward
Lens: Normal

Early or late lighting is essential in flat desert areas. Here, warmth of afternoon light adds an additional color to a monochrome subject. The camel drivers carry tourists to the pyramids from the car parking area. These colorful people and their camels are also wonderful models lending foreground interest.

MYTHOLOGY RUNS LIKE FIRE IN THE VEINS OF THE GREEKS. Even today it is difficult for them to untangle the snagged skein of myth and fact which are the bases of Greek history.

As to the fact, Greece geologically is a rocky rough-hewn country. It is apropos that this stone has been the medium of many of its cultural gifts to the world in architecture and sculpture. Upon a rocky butte in the midst of Athens is its citadel, the Acropolis. Even though vandals have desecrated its original majesty, it still belongs to the architectural cameos of the world. A superlative in marble is the Parthenon, a pure Doric temple, simple and solid, patterned after earlier temples of brick and timber. Pericles, the statesman and orator who led the Athenians for thirty years, persuaded them to build the noble temple to Athena in 447 B.C. at a cost to their treasury which staggered these Greeks.

Marble quarried by slaves from the mountain Pentelicus (visible from the Acropolis) was hauled by many oxen to the site and lifted by derricks, blocks and tackles. Phidias, the most famous sculptor in history, supervised the erection of the various temples of the Acropolis which in early days was a place of refuge. He directed the construction of the Parthenon and the erection of its great columns — separate stones shaped into drums or sections by lathes. The top drum and the lowest drum of each pillar were fluted before the pillar was erected. The middle sections were carved after the column was in place so that the upper and lower flutings would be correctly joined. Engineers, knowing the distortion which straight lines in such a huge building would produce to the normal eye, used subtle curves and leaning pillars to create an optical illusion of correctness. Skillful techniques plus the rare sculpturing of metopes, friezes and pediments produced the incomparable Parthenon, Temple of Athena, Virgin Goddess.

As to myth, the Parthenon was built to house the 30-foot wooden statue of Athena, overlaid with gold. Athena's father, Zeus, swallowed her pregnant mother, fearing his own unborn child might someday supercede him in power. In so doing he did not destroy her, for Prometheus (who stole fire from the Gods to give to man) split the head of Zeus, and Zeus' daughter Athena emerged fully armed. Athena, the most revered of Athenian goddesses, was not only a goddess of war but of peace and wisdom, a virgin with mental and moral stability. We find she also had skill in the homely arts of weaving, shoemaking, spinning and shipbuilding.

There was a second statue of Athena just inside the Propylaea, the entrance of the Acropolis, a gigantic image of the goddess built of metal collected by the Greeks at Marathon after they had routed the Persians in 490 B.C.

During its checkered existence of two milleniums the Parthenon has housed a Christian church and an Islamic mosque. A minaret added to this unorthodox mosque must have been an incongruous touch to pure Doric architecture.

The death blow for the Acropolis came when the Parthenon, used as a Turkish ammunition warehouse, was the target in 1687 of a Venetian shell which shattered the building. In 1830 archaeologists began restoration of the Acropolis and, fortunately for the world, this work is still in progress.

Time: Late evening or total darkness
Direction: North
Lens: Long

A rare opportunity offers picture possibilities when late evening light and artificial lighting can change a monochromatic subject into a colorful one. A multi-exposure technique can be used, though a balanced time exposure often will achieve outstanding results.

Barley Mill / Mykonos, Greece

FLY OVER THE AEGEAN SEA SOME SPARKLING DAY. LOOK down on its blue waters coated with the sun's gold dust and you will see that Zeus, King of the Grecian gods, has carelessly broadcast a handful of white marble chips from Pentelicus over the surface of the sea. Or so it looked to me, gazing down from the welkin upon this archipelago of the Cyclades, Dodecanese and Sporades Islands.

Today these islands have become the "mecca of meccas" for travelers. Cruises and tours under many nomenclatures visit them as well as sailing enthusiasts, private yachts and individual travelers. Fortunately, these islands escaped destruction in World War II. There was no advantage to anyone in bombing them.

For almost four hundred years — from 1522 — the Turks controlled the islands, demanding payment of taxes from the islanders in return for a measure of autonomy. The Italians wrested the islands from the Turks in 1912, and only after Italy was defeated in World War II did she surrender the last of her strongholds here, the island of Rhodes. Much poverty resulted from these two jurisdictions, causing many Greeks to leave their islands for other countries. Mykonos is one of the Cyclades (from the Greek *kyklos* meaning circle) which form a peripheral protection for the sacred island of Delos, apocryphal birthplace of Apollo and his twin sister, Artemis. A more substantial reason for protecting Delos was the rich treasury of the Athenians which was deposited there for safekeeping.

Mykonos — without the mythology and antiquity of Delos — is a typical Aegean island, but dressed in its Sunday best seven days a week. Its whitewashed houses and narrow streets with small flower-boxed balconies, its seaside fishermen and shops, its postwar hotels as well as its friendly inhabitants leave the traveler with very pleasant memories. A few of its many former windmills are left, white stucco towers with 40-foot wind wheels. Directly under the thatched roof we saw barley ground under hefty millstones turned by half-reefed canvas sails on the radial arms of the wheel.

In 1952 why would anyone wish to go to the Greek Islands? Unheard of! Were we completely berserk? A kind Greek friend in Athens encountered one stone wall after another in his search for a captain who would take us to any or all of the little islands on his small inter-island ship. But we broke the ice.

Today Mykonos with its electricity, modern hotels, cafes and shops is a far cry from the still-dark harbor where we crawled into a dinghy to reach the shore. The hotel manager in 1952 met us and walked us with our bags to the only hotel on Mykonos, lighted by a kerosene lantern in the window. He showed us up a narrow tread-worn stairway to a cold bare bedroom with two cots and one candle. We were the only "griegos" on the island. Why, he wondered, had we come? Today he knows. Other Americans have found it and made it one of the most popular places of the Aegean archipelago, that "much shattered old land block almost entirely submerged" in the Greek sea.

Time: Early morning
Direction: Southwest
Lens: Normal

An all-white subject in dazzling brilliant sunlight is in itself a challenge. Like photographing snow, I recommend reading a neutral surface and giving the subject about 100 percent less exposure. Even this approximation should be safeguarded with several bracketed exposures. This subject will lend itself to good lighting throughout the entire day. An approaching storm made my decision easy, yet one should not overlook the possibility of a spectacular sunset with such a subject as a silhouette.

Lindos / Rhodes, Greece

THE ACROPOLIS AT LINDOS WAS QUIET AND LONELY AS WE stood alone, looking seaward, at the foot of several remaining Doric columns of still another Temple of Athena. Not a nostalgic loneliness, but one of peace away from the insatiable crowds of the world. Over the edge of the sheer cliffs we could see two bays that winged this hilltop, indentations of the blue Mediterranean. The story persists that the Apostle Paul beached here on his way from Miletus to Jerusalem, a logical landfall for him.

On this rocky promontory are fragments of an old Byzantine church and several halls of Crusaders, reminders of the history and architectural achievements of various invaders. At the base of the stone stairway leading to this Acropolis carved in bas-relief from the rock itself, is an ancient trireme. This is unusual because ships are not commonly found in Greek sculpture. The Greeks were more concerned about immortalizing themselves and their deities.

The third side of the promontory slopes down to the town of Lindos. A few years after World War II, even with the generous and appreciated assistance of the "Marshall States" — as they referred to the United States then — the men of Lindos could not support their families on the rocky farms of the area and emigrated to North Africa to find work. A smiling lonely woman, keeper of the home and hearth, welcomed us warmly to her doorstep and then into her one-room home. The family genealogy hung on the wall, a series of chipped and precious Rhodian pottery plates covering a span of several hundred years; a new plate is produced at each birth.

Half way to the ceiling and protruding from the walls there were two wide shelves on which beds were neatly stacked with mattresses and blankets. At night the whole family climbed a ladder and shared the two beds. We could think of several advantages of this arrangement, warmth and safety among them. One day as we were driving through the island of Rhodes, our Turkish *cicerone* had explained the heavy high boots worn by the women working in the fields by "women please very much serpent." High beds would discourage visiting snakes.

Xenophon of 430 B.C. — the Greek sophist, soldier, traveler and writer — must have had Lindos in mind when he wrote "there is beauty in order, even in pots and pans." The small courtyard kitchens here, primitive by city standards, sparkle with their burnished pots and pans. Even more memorable than the Acropolis of Lindos were the quaint streets and courtyards paved with smooth matched stones, slightly larger than a proverbial pebble, like sugar-coated almonds. These are placed on the narrow edges of the stones, embedded compactly in cement. It seemed a herculean task alone to have collected these stones of such perfect symmetry sculptured by the sea through the ages, but of such is Lindos.

Time: Afternoon
Direction: East
Lens: Normal

The simplicity of Lindos sets it apart from all other Greek subjects. This acropolis is some 600 feet above the blue Mediterranean and, though several good vantage points are available, one should be aware of the cliffs — and not take that one more step backward as one unfortunate camera fan did! Most people are transported up the hill on a donkey guided by one of the local citizens who take turns transporting guests to the several places of interest.

The Blue Mosque / Istanbul, Turkey

WHEN THE OTTOMAN SULTAN AHMED I HAD HIS "INCREDU-lous temple" built in Istanbul (1609–1616 A.D.) he committed the unholy error of building six minarets, equal in number to the minarets of Islam's mother mosque, the Ka'bah in Mecca. Incensed by this profanation, Islam's faithful then added a seventh minaret to Mecca's Holy of Holies. The Blue Mosque, as it is popularly known, gives those of us forbidden entrance to Mecca a satisfying taste of minarets.

Architecturally there are four different types of minarets in various Moslem countries. They have been described by travelers as candles, spindles, arrows of the sky, but to me there is no synonym for minaret. It is unique. From this symbolic lighthouse of the mosque, the muezzin projects his voice (now with modern megaphone) above the hubbub of life below to remind the faithful Moslem that it is time to stop in his tracks and give thanks to Allah, his Maker.

A visitor gazing on the multiple domes and half domes of the Blue Mosque commented that it looked to him as though the huge central dome had just pupped!

The inside of a mosque is seldom ornate due to the fact that the sacred scriptures of Islam — the Koran — forbid "idolatry or deification of created beings." However, the Arabic script incorporated in the blue tiles covering the inside of the mosque is so fluid in form that it is decorative in itself. During the seventeenth century, Nicaea was one of several Turkish cities in Asia Minor that produced fine pottery, and these blue tiles are believed to be Nicaean. Through the clear glass windows, light floods the great spaces of the Blue Mosque and accentuates the fading indigo on its pillars, domes and walls. The usual Moslem prayer niche (mihrab) indicating the direction of Mecca, the elaborately carved marble pulpit (mimbar), heavy wrought iron chandeliers suspended from the ceiling by a spiderweb of wires, and oriental prayer rugs equip the mosque.

Sultan Ahmed I may not be recorded as one of the greatest of the Ottoman rulers, but his Blue Mosque has been a treasured landmark in Istanbul for over 350 years.

To put Istanbul into proper perspective, we might encapsule its history into five major periods; first, founded by the Greek named Byzas in 657 B.C. from whom the name Byzantium originated; second, ruled by the Macedonian King Alexander the Great (334-323 B.C.) and still called Byzantium; third, under the rule of the Christian Roman Emperor Constantine who moved his capital from Rome to Byzantium and changed its name to Constantinople, which was held by the Romans for over eleven centuries from 330 to 1453 A.D.; fourth, conquered and held by the Ottoman Turks under Osman and the name of the city changed to Istanbul; fifth, as the major city of the modern Republic of Turkey established in 1923. The great reformer and "benevolent dictator" Mustafa Ataturk, as President moved the Turkish capital to Ankara in Asia Minor.

Istanbul, no longer a capital, is still a city of imperishable romance, history and modern interest.

Time: Morning
Direction: South
Lens: Normal

This magnificent mosque, one of many in the area, lends itself best of all to good photography. Its location makes it outstanding from several directions, for it is not hemmed in by surrounding buildings as is so often the case with mosques elsewhere. Flowers are best in spring though an attempt is made to keep the park in flowers throughout the summer.

Old Dubrovnik / Yugoslavia

A STRIP OF ADRIATIC SEACOAST 200 MILES LONG AND ONLY 35 miles wide was for centuries the elongated country called Dalmatia. When in 1918 it became part of Yugoslavia, the name of its most important town — Ragusa — was changed to the Slavic name Dubrovnik. This is one of the simplest Slavic names to pronounce, but if you are unfamiliar with the Balto-Slavic language (and who isn't!), give a wide berth to such "simple" names as Erd and Krka. Because, to get an organized idea of language here as well as history, one needs an electronic computer with a read-out system attached to it.

Enjoy Dubrovnik without full knowledge of its harried past! If you are a specialist of walled cities of early medieval times, here is a superb one to add to your list. Within this well-preserved walled city with quilted red-tiled roofs, are narrow streets, convents, monasteries, churches, schools, theatres and even a naval academy. This was a great maritime center once with two thousand ships at its command. This strong maritime tradition has continued and one can see a present-day regatta that is delightful.

Although an earthquake destroyed part of Dubrovnik in 1667 the city looks much as it did 500 years ago. The visitor is transported backwards half a millenium in time.

Dubrovnik, protruding into the Adriatic precisely like a bent elbow, is the destination of many ships and boats, both in the Adriatic and Mediterranean. Sailing enthusiasts set a course for Dubrovnik. In ancient days all visitors to Ragusa (Dubrovnik) were required to pass a physical inspection in lazarets outside of the city walls, for the city was carefully guarded against the epidemics and plagues of that day.

Now you will be welcomed without this annoying delay not only in Dubrovnik but everywhere. For according to a colorful pamphlet issued by Yugoslavia's Tourist Association and from which I quote with some slight reservations, you will find "opportunity for rest and enjoyment in some 2000 seaside resorts along the coast and on the islands." Take your pick.

Time: Morning
Direction: Westward
Lens: Long

Here a whole city is the objective, though many close-ups are available. Along the Mediterranean haze builds up and often clarity of the air is not as good as would be desired. Lucky is the photographer who can be around after a good shower cleans the air for a few days. The nearby hillside offers numerous vantage points during the entire day.

Turkish Bridge / Mostar, Yugoslavia

WHEN YOU ARE IN DUBROVNIK YOU WILL WANT TO DRIVE inland about one hundred miles into the rocky country of Hercegovina to see the town of Mostar with its simple single-arch bridge spanning the Naretva River. The Naretva flows through deep gorges and there is a sparse population along this waterway. But Mostar has been here for centuries. If you want to "bone up" on the involved history, intrigue and government of Bosnia-Hercegovina, Sarejevo, and the like, take an encyclopedia along with you.

The Turks came to Mostar, Hercegovina, in 1463 and stayed here a full four hundred years. It was undoubtedly the Turks who built the bridge in the fifteenth century which today intrigues many photographers. Some claim that the Romans built its foundations — a claim that could also be possible.

The Mohammedan mosques and Turkish houses contrast strongly with the buildings of the medieval walled city of Dubrovnik. Mostar, possibly because of its inaccessibility, is a much more rural and primitive city than Dubrovnik, which was always a city of intellectual and cultural background. The Turks militantly brought their religion, Islam, with them to Mostar and most of the inhabitants accepted it. Thus there are Moslems in Mostar as well as Roman Catholics and members of the Eastern Orthodox church.

There is a feeling of a light-opera setting here, and with a good script writer the old bridge might play a significant role in the *most old* city, meaning Mostar.

Time: Late afternoon
Direction: Southeast
Lens: Normal

This Turkish arch is quite likely one of the most picturesque bridges to be found. It is photogenic from both sides and from several vantage points. To photograph it from the north in order to include the colored tableware of an outdoor restaurant one must wait until about 4:00 P.M. before sunshine strikes the north or upstream side of the arch. Too much later and the vivid color of the water changes for the worse. Weather is generally favorable though I had to wait over a second day due to one stubborn cloud that just wouldn't drift on.

The Kremlin / Moscow, Russia

THE KREMLIN ON THE MOSCOW RIVER STILL REPRESENTS the heartbeat of Russia despite the fact that the czars and nobles who built it have been eliminated.

If you had visited the Kremlin (citadel) early in the twelfth century you would have found it not much more than a muddy trading post enclosed by a shaky pine-log stockade. Its houses and churches were built of wood and heated by simple wood stoves. The Kremlin became the nucleus of a city which grew up around it, called Moscow. Walled areas were built around the walled Kremlin, one after another, like the rings emanating from a pebble dropped into still waters. Just inside the outermost wooden walls, in the Wooden City, lived the serfs and laborers. Within the next ring of walls lived the aristocrats and some of the merchants in the White City. Next came the area nearest to the walled Kremlin and Red Square — the area known as Kitai Gorod where lived the merchants and craftsmen.

Grand Duke Ivan Kalita — old "moneybags" — by his Machiavellian intrigues and clever dealing with the Mogul rulers of Russia at that time, was able to make the Kremlin the seat of government, and the principality of Moscow became increasingly important. Ivan refortified the triangularly shaped 65 acres of citadel — the Kremlin — with stone walls. Through the centuries the city burgeoned. It became the Holy See, spiritual headquarters of the Russian Orthodox Church, thus bringing church and state into close association.

While Columbus was discovering America in 1492, the present crenelated walls were built around the Kremlin. During Czarist regimes many splendid structures were crowded onto this acropolis — largely buildings of Byzantine style with ogee roofs and gilded domes. The great Bell Tower of Ivan the Great, churches, palaces, apartments, an arsenal, as well as many treasures and trappings of royalty still exist here to be seen by the visitor today.

After the deposition of Czar Nicholas and the Revolution of 1917, these beautiful buildings ceased to be functional and were immobilized by the Soviet Government. Fortunately for history, they were not destroyed and were opened to the public in 1955. One fine modern building has been added, perhaps somewhat inconsistent architecturally with the rest of the Kremlin. Called the Palace of Congress, it was built of gleaming white marble and much glass, and is used as a great conference hall, and for film festivals and similar events.

The Kremlin in Moscow has always been Russia's seat of power except for the two hundred years when St. Petersburg was the capital. Still the government headquarters for the U.S.S.R., it is where their chief executives and leaders hold forth. From the river view the Grand Kremlin Palace, the meeting place of the Grand Soviet, is conspicuous.

Time: Afternoon
Direction: Northeast
Lens: Long — normal

The Moscow River forms a natural border for the Kremlin — its walls, museums and buildings of state. From two bridges one can obtain vantage points of interest, and if a cloudy sky is clearing after a storm so much the better. Exposure should be based upon an average subject, letting the golden domes accent with their brilliance. Color is not to be found everywhere in Russia's two largest cities. Buildings are rather monotone, natural cement, stone or mellowed paint. This, of course, makes the more colorful Kremlin and Red Square outstanding, yet their immensity also makes them difficult subjects.

Red Square / Moscow, Russia

RED SQUARE IS A LARGE RECTANGULAR COBBLESTONED AREA about one half the size of the Kremlin and is adjacent to the pink brick walls of the Kremlin itself. The predominant color here does not give it the name "Red" nor does the red Russian flag have anything to do with the name. The Russian word for beautiful also means red.

While the Kremlin still lay within a wooden stockade made of pine logs, Red Square was an ill-smelling, bickering, noisy marketplace at the crossroads of the trade routes. Its focal point, "the umbilicus of the world," was a stone rostrum from which public speeches were made and blessings given. At the same time public tortures were performed here and heads literally rolled, red with blood on this spot. When it became red in a beautiful sense of the word is uncertain.

Today and for centuries it has been the great open stage of the Russian Capital on which millions of Russians have played parts in military displays, revolutions, festivals, massive gatherings to hear official speeches and of course the famous May Day Parade.

Stand in the center of the square where only foot traffic is allowed and face the Kremlin's towered walls. The unadorned boxy red polished granite Mausoleum of Lenin is before you, hugging the wall of the Kremlin. You are immediately aware of it due to the long queue of people before it awaiting admittance to this hallowed necropolis. Russians return time after time to look upon the body of their lionized leader. Having been cautioned to be breathlessly silent upon entering the darkened crypt, it was bloodcurdling when a small babe in arms cried out in fear and panic. The whole building was suffused with loud hisses from the glaring guards stationed at every turn. Stalin — Russia's leader for 29 years — was exhibited lying beside Lenin in this tomb until his downgrading began in 1961 when his body was removed and placed under an unadorned stone slab behind Lenin's tomb. Even to mention Stalin's name to a foreigner is anathema to any Russian today.

Back in the center of Red Square, in the same position, St. Basil's Cathedral is at your left — a building so fascinating and so ludicrous one doesn't know whether to be awed or to laugh. This collection of mongrel domes facetted by colored tiles covers a maze of chapels connected by tunnels. It has been called "Byzantine Renaissance and Tatar design" if it must have a name. The neurotic Ivan the Terrible built this phantasm to crown his achievement in conquering the Tatars in Kazan. This victory in 1551 was the first defeat of the Tatars and resulted in making the Volga River a part of Russia.

Behind you on the square is Gum's, the enormous and equally famous arcaded department store which is run by the government. This emporium is located in the area which, in the days of the walled districts, was called Kitai Gorod, inhabited by the merchants and craftsmen of Moscow.

To your right at the far end of the Square, opposite St. Basil's, stands the State Historical Museum built on the site of Moscow's old university.

Time: Late afternoon
Direction: East
Lens: Normal

Here a tourist for the first time is a bit timid and tends to lose valuable photographic time. Weather too can be a deterrent, yet the gloomiest day can clear as it did for me a few moments before sundown. Scaffolding can be expected wherever there is a tower or temple, museum or statue. Always they are disappointing and ugly. The tourist is permitted to photograph any public building and tourist attraction.

Exhibition of Economic Achievements / Moscow, Russia

THE POLYTECHNIC MUSEUM OF MOSCOW WHICH EARLY SCIentists established in 1872 to display natural history, ethnology, anthropology and to promote various branches of scientific knowledge, has grown today into a handsome group of halls and pavilions surrounded by fountains, gardens and gilded sculpturing. A permanent sort of fair, a display of all things Russian, draws millions of visitors each year to view the historical past, the present-day successes, and the communistic plans and promises of the future. As in many industrial museums of the world, there are working models of machines, farm equipment, engineering projects, mining displays, computers, and similar objects among the 100,000 items in its collections.

Architectural curiosity alone would lure the traveler in Moscow to visit this exhibition to see the exteriors as well as the interiors of some 50 buildings spread over 500 acres. Here again is the repetitive "Stalinist Gothic" type of architecture, but it is seen here on a smaller scale than in many larger buildings spread throughout Moscow — pyramidal skyscrapers topped with towers and spires. There are pavilions also representing the various republics of the Soviet Socialist Union and various nationalities.

Quite naturally, the zenith of attractions is the pavilion which houses the achievements of the U.S.S.R. in outer space — rockets, satellites and the like. Especially dear to the Russian people's hearts because it was a "first" is the exhibit of their rocket which hit the moon in September 1959.

Time: Afternoon
Direction: Southeast
Lens: Medium wide angle

This water fountain is one of the most impressive I have seen. Its gold-leafed figures representing each of the Soviet Union's states in a setting of buildings commemorating triumphs or achievements cannot but catch the photographer's eye. On an overcast and cloudy day the gold reflects more evenly than in brilliant sunlight. Normally the fountains are turned on from noon until four o'clock and it can be disconcerting to have the fountains go off just when you are ready to expose. These are the subjects most often photographed. I suggest one save his desire for human documentary photographs for other, less politically sensitive countries.

The Admiralty
Church of the Transfiguration / Leningrad, Russia
St. Isaac's Cathedral

WITH HIS PROFOUND DESIRE TO EXPOSE RUSSIA TO EURO-
pean progress, the tall, ambitious, powerful Czar Peter
the Great took a negative and transformed it into a positive
within a ten-year period (1703–12) when he created the city of
Petersburg (now Leningrad) out of miasmic swamps at the
edge of the Baltic Sea. This he made the Russian capital and it
so remained for over two hundred years until the Bolsheviks
returned the capital to Moscow in 1918.

Peter the Great was Russia's first modern Czar and in his
compulsion to Europeanize Russia, he even insisted that men
shave their old Russian beards or pay a tax to wear one. He
changed the Russian calendar which began in September "when
apples are ripe" to coincide with the European calendar beginning in January. Undoubtedly, when he removed women from
seclusion he had no idea that today Russian women would not
only outnumber the men but would perform 55 percent of all
of the labor and become known as "the heroic sex." Three out
of four doctors in Russia today, for example, are women.

Leningrad (St. Petersburg, then in 1914, Petrograd) shows
strong European features in its architecture. The Admiralty,
built on the Neva River, is a looming landmark with its gold
dome and spire. After Peter was defeated by the Tatars near
the Black Sea in 1695 for lack of sea power, he immediately
built a fleet of transports and barges and returned to defeat his
enemies. Later, when he built St. Petersburg, a low wooden
building sufficed for his first real ship-building slips on the banks
of the Neva — and from here Russia's first fleet was launched.
The present Admiralty built in the early 1800s is in no sense a
construction ways but a handsome memorial to Russia's naval
achievements where no keels are laid other than possibly some
governmental careers.

The Church of the Transfiguration was the chapel of a
regiment of Circassian soldiers known as the Preobrazhensky
Guards, many of whom were Muslims. This probably accounts
for the mosque-like domes on this church in Leningrad. A fierce,
sturdy group of mountain men, these soldiers were used by the
Russians to fight against Turkey (1828–29) and, after Russia's
victory, 102 cannons were utilized as an appropriate fence
around the church, the cannons being placed muzzle down as an
indication of cessation of war.

St. Isaac's Cathedral was at one time a symbol of Russia's
religious spirit. It is no longer used as a church. Today U.S.S.R.
calls it a museum, a monument to Russia's former religion. One
of the magnificent cathedrals of the world, its golden dome has
been compared to that of St. Peter's in Rome, St. Paul's in
London and the dome of the Capitol of the United States. Here
is massive and dramatic architecture, a cathedral unique in that
it has four handsome entrances — one on each side of the building — with steps made of Finnish granite leading up to the
porticoes supported by 55-foot polished columns. Within this
Orthodox church, which had a capacity of 13,000 people, remain
some of the large icons. Its walls are inlaid with lapis lazuli and
malachite showing its once rare beauty and fine workmanship.

Time: Morning
Direction: Northwest
Lens: Wide angle

*Future visitors should fare a bit better than I did, for nearly all the notable build-
ings of Leningrad were covered with scaffolding during the summer of 1967.
They were being scraped and painted for the fall celebration of the Fiftieth
Anniversary of Russia's Revolution. Even the Hermitage was hidden by steel lat-
tice. The Admiralty, facing east, and the eastern and southern front of St. Isaac's
and the Church of the Transfiguration, respectively, are all most photogenic
with morning light. Though an Intourist guide is quite helpful, it may take a bit of
persuasion to alter her usual routine route to the places of interest. Probably a
quick tour for orientation would be advisable, with a return to buildings of striking interest. However, a serious photographer will always make a picture at the
first opportunity, never waiting to return later at a more convenient time. It
often rains, or a construction crew can commence a restoration project, or a
truck may break down right in front of your best camera location (this happened
in front of the world-famous Raffles Hotel in Singapore). In Russia, as anywhere, ask people for permission if you wish to photograph them. Avoid pictures
showing women working at various hard labor trades. Ask your guide if in doubt.*

THE ADMIRALTY

CHURCH OF THE TRANSFIGURATION

ST. ISAAC'S CATHEDRAL

Cathedral on Senate Square / Helsinki, Finland

SUOMI, SIBELIUS, SAARINEN, SMORGASBORD, SAUNA ARE A few of the sibilants one can toss off the tongue and instantly identify Finland, called Suomi by the Finns.

In spite of Finland's ultra-modern examples of architecture both in Finland and around the world, the great white-domed Empire-style Cathedral of Helsinki, poised high above the floor of Senate Square, will never be superceded as the Grand Dame of Finland. The Cathedral was built between 1830 and 1840 after Helsinki had become the capital of Finland which was then a Russian Duchy.

Sweden ceded Finland to Russia in 1809 after which the Russians moved the capital from Turku or Abo on the west coast of Finland to Helsinki, closer to the parental eye of the Czars. Long before this, the Swedish crusader Eric IX had conquered the Finns in 1155. Sweden, then a more civilized country than Finland, had given the Finns civil rights. Under Sweden's democratic King Haakon they also had been given the right to vote. The Republic of Finland was born out of the Russian Revolution in 1917 at which time Finland established itself as a parliamentary democracy.

The earliest migrants to Finland were Ugrian tribes coming from the south across the Gulf of Finland. With the intrusion of the Swedes, both Swedish and Finnish (a most difficult Ural-Altaic language similar to Hungarian) were used and even now Finland is a bilingual country. Present-day Finns are a mixture of the early dark Slavs and the fair Teutons of Sweden.

A great race of hardy athletes, the Finns anticipated hosting the Olympic Games in 1940, building a peerless modern stadium for the event in Helsinki. War — again — delayed its use until 1952.

Although Finland is a relatively young nation, it is expanding rapidly in its culture, sciences and arts. With all of its budding modernity, it is our impression that the big white Cathedral on Senate Square will never be replaced by a modern building for it is cherished as a symbol — above all architectural achievements.

Time: Morning
Direction: North
Lens: Small picture — long; large picture — wide angle

My first impression was that this is a clean, peaceful city. Couples in native costume were entering the church that dominates the heart of the city. The parks were well kept, giving the city a feeling of serenity. Helsinki is a moderately photogenic city with interesting small harbors, churches, docks and the like.

Old Stockholm / Sweden

ALL OF THE SCANDINAVIAN COUNTRIES LEAVE THE TRAVELER with a feeling of well-being, freshness and a desire to return to them. Stimulating, honest, clean, vigorous, progressive and cultured are these people who balance the scale of living in favor of the good things of life.

Cities like Stockholm embody this mode of living. Old Stockholm is the eye of Sweden, having been so for seven centuries since the Swedish statesman Burger Jarl established a fortress in 1250 on a small island at the neck of Malar Lake. This body of fresh water, which flows into the Baltic, extends westward for 75 miles. There are thousands of islands cradled in its fluid arms. Over the years, Stockholm outgrew its small citadel, crept onto various islands, and fanned out onto the shores of Lake Malar. Old Stockholm is still the magnet even though new Stockholm has enveloped and surrounded it with modern buildings, industry and art forms.

The Goths were the first settlers, living in Skåne, southern Sweden. Gothenburg, The Gota Canal, Gothland, are remnants of their habitation here. Sweden along with Norway was united under the rule of Denmark until Sweden's liberator, Gustavus Vasa, led a revolt, freed the country, and became Sweden's first monarch in 1523.

The Palace of the Swedish monarchs is in Old Stockholm. Here they were crowned. Under today's constitutional monarchy, the old silver throne is used only once a year when the King opens Parliament. Nearby is the Riddarholm Church with its lacy spire within which four hundred years of Swedish kings are buried.

From Skåne's waving grain fields and stern old castles in southern Sweden, drive northward through Lake Vättern country with Viking memories, north again to its University and great Cathedral at Uppsala, then to its crystal Lake Siljan where Falun red barns dot the countryside; head on north up its Ångerman River where rafts of logs are on their way south downstream to the pulp and sawmills. Sample an immaculate Swedish train and continue northward to Lapland for an ultimate experience under the midnight sun.

Time: Afternoon
Direction: East
Lens: Normal — long

Fortunately, so far this old and colorful part of modern Stockholm has been preserved as much as possible. Nearby tall buildings are rising, while the inevitable freeway interchanges and all that is common to new growth edge ever closer. This view is from the city hall. The tower is open only from 11:00 A.M. until 4:00 P.M.

Geiranger Fiord / Norway

GEIRANGER FIORD IS ONE OF HUNDREDS OF SPACES BETWEEN the ragged teeth of the comb which is the seacoast of Norway (Norge). Only slightly smaller than California, Norway's coastline "as the crow flies" is a thousand miles in length. While California has very few harbors, Norway is surfeited with bays, inlets, and *viks* formed by the channeling of glaciers and rivers born on the craggy backbone of Norway's high mountains and which move relentlessly to sea level in the Atlantic Ocean and Norwegian Sea. Geiranger Fiord threads through singularly precipitous walls, some 6000 feet high, over which plunge The Seven Sisters as individual water falls. The Bridal Veil is another falls of phenomenal beauty.

If you are a climber, it is an exhilarating experience to follow the foothpath up the mountainside and look down, like the Norse god Odin, on the pygmies of mankind below you. You may come upon the summer grazing plot of the Norseman's cattle. The herder who lives up here all summer with the cattle, each day sends his milk in buckets to the valley floor over long cables.

Fiords or *viks* have always dominated the lives of Norwegians for the sea has been their source of livelihood. Farm lands in Norway are minimal. Fishing, whaling, and other maritime pursuits have been the lifeblood of these people.

Between 700 and 1100 A.D. roving bands of Norsemen, Vikings, ranged the seas in their shallow, high-prowed wooden boats, pillaging and destroying seacoast towns and settlements with ferocity — sometimes establishing settlements of their own. From the *viks*, where they anchored ships at home, came, of course, the name Vikings. Planting their spring crops in their homeland, they departed for foreign shores under the protection of their mythological gods. There was scarcely a European country untouched by the fierce and unexpected shore raids of these Vikings who attacked with swiftness and stealth, plundered towns and returned home in time to harvest their crops. The north coast of France bears their name, Normandy. For 300 years they were a scourge. Explorers also in their fragile boats, they put their signature on England, Scotland, Ireland, Iceland, Greenland, and many islands and christened their landfall in North America in 1000 A.D. as Vinland.

Norwegian folklore tells of a warrior so valiant and of such ferocity that he fought minus armor of any kind. His name was Berserker and he had a dozen sons who fought likewise, thus establishing the word "berserk" as a term to be applied to many unbalanced people of the world.

From the fearless and courageous ancient Viking stock have come some of the world's greatest explorers. In 1893 Fridtjof Nansen in his specially constructed wooden ship, the *Fram,* explored the north polar regions with his ship frozen into the polar ice for two years. Roald Amundsen in 1911 was the first man to reach the South Pole — on foot — and in 1929 still another Norwegian, Bernt Balchen, flew Admiral Byrd over the South Pole without landing.

The terror of the Vikings is history, but the descendents of those ruddy men are the sturdy and courageous Norwegians of today.

Time: Morning
Direction: West
Lens: Long

Here again is mountainous country and the unpredictable weather. It can snow in July, so there is the possibility of photographs with the greens of summer and fresh snow. Be prepared to wait. It's beautiful country. Exposure is a compromise favoring the greens rather than the white clouds and snow. One should scout the area for picture possibilities during poor weather so that the most can be made of sunny intervals.

Stock Exchange / Copenhagen, Denmark

Superlatives are seldom entirely correct, but the statement that Denmark is the oldest existing kingdom in the world seems justified. In the eighth century Denmark had kings who claimed they were descendents of their mythological gods, and kings have ruled Denmark continuously since then. Their red flag with the white Latin cross quadrisecting it has been Denmark's national emblem for almost 750 years, ever since King Waldemar envisioned a white cross emblazoned upon the red sky of battle and, victorious in 1219, established the flag.

The rooftop view of Copenhagen cannot be mistaken for that of any other city. Heavy copper roofs green with the patina of age are common elsewhere. But nowhere else can one find the identifying spire of the twisted tails of four dragons topping the ornately gabled roof of the Copenhagen Stock Exchange, the Bourse. King Christian IV, who ascended the Danish throne in 1588, a most energetic man even at sixty-seven years of age, not only renewed the fortifications of his city but also, with an eye to encouraging trade and exchange of goods in his Kjoben-havn — Merchants Haven — or Copenhagen, built the Bourse in 1619 as a merchandise exchange. Within its halls were booths and warehouses of merchants. Later Christian sold it to an ambitious Kjobenhavn merchant. In time it reverted to royal holdings but, as the economy progressed, a fraternity of merchants — the Merchants' Guild — acquired it.

This Bourse too is classified as "oldest" — the oldest building to be constructed as an exchange. Today it is still an exchange but trade goods and merchandise have been supplanted by stocks and bonds. The Copenhagen Stock Exchange is an organized stock and bond market where only members may buy and sell. Membership requires a broker's license and, to assure each member's responsibility, a deposit must be made.

As for trade, Copenhagen since 1894 has been a "free port" where goods may be shuffled or shifted and cargoes transshipped without penalty of import taxes.

Hans Christian Andersen's "wonderful, wonderful Copenhagen" is still a rare source of superfine merchandise. There is a flagrant temptation to the traveler to "wait until you get to Copenhagen" to buy fine porcelain, glass, silver, furs and furniture. Let us not forget to relish Copenhagen's gigantic open-faced Danish sandwiches and its delicious Carlsberg beer.

Since 1876 profits from Captain Jacobsen's Carlsberg Brewery (named for his son Carl) have been the basis of the income of the Carlsberg Foundation to promote research and publication — perhaps a forerunner of the Rockefeller, Ford and other great foundations.

Time: Morning
Direction: Southwest
Lens: Normal

Copenhagen's Stock Exchange and nearby civic buildings can be photographed in morning light. Fast-moving clouds from the west offer an everchanging sky. This, of course, can be a forewarning of complete overcast and rain. I would again advise one to "make hay while the sun shines." Sunday morning is usually the best day for avoiding cars parked in front of public buildings. Additional obstacles are the ever-present neon signs and power wires where once a fruit or flower stand offered a beautiful foreground. Yet these discouraging obstacles often force one to choose another view point, often resulting in a better picture. The "Little Mermaid" visited by most first visitors to Copenhagen faces westward and is an afternoon photograph.

Canal / Bruges, Belgium

THE FLEMISH CITY OF BRUGES, LIKE OTHER LOWLAND CITIES, is a town of waterways and canals. Flanders, although it referred to Bruges and its immediate surroundings in ancient days, is today a northern province of Belgium and its sandy seacoast is the northern border of Belgium on the North Sea. Flanders extends slightly into Holland, eastward, and more considerably into France to the west.

Bruges is an example of a thriving fourteenth-century city that was an inland seaport and great trading center, cultured and wealthy and administered by nobility. However, it was finally isolated from the sea by the forces of nature. Ships used to ascend the Zwin River from the North Sea to within three miles of Bruges where goods were transported up a lesser waterway and delivered to Bruges for sale and reexportation. The powerful Hanseatic League of merchants had interests here. But drifting sands filled in the lowlands between Bruges and the North Sea, completely clogging and finally eliminating the delta channels which led inland from the sea to Bruges.

If the burghers of Bruges had been courageous enough to build a canal directly from the city to the North Sea — an idea promoted by a Flemish painter — its history might have been greatly altered. Many years later such a canal was cut from Bruges to Ostend on the North Sea, but by then Bruges had settled into complacency and continued to be the medieval town it is today.

Neat homes with peaked tiled roofs and picturesque corbie-stepped gables line the streets alongside the quiet flower-bordered canals of Bruges. There is a plaintiveness and tranquility about Bruges — even to its legendary swans — that charm travelers more than the bustle of other cities. From a prosperous trading center where merchants gathered to transact their business in the house of Van der Buerze (thought possibly to be the origin of the word "bourse"), sand dunes changed this Cinderella of commerce back into her simple dress and a quiet way of living.

Bruges wears a mellow halo, like the caps of the Flemish lacemakers in Bruges, and there are even "gossip mirrors" on the window frames of some of the old houses, the front-door peepholes of that day. As in the days when nobles ruled, there is still a Count of Flanders. Flemish is spoken here and in much of northern Belgium, French in the south.

The great square belfry in the market square with its resonant carillon of forty-seven bells is the pride of Bruges. Bells, like windmills, are part of the romance of the Old World. Do not miss a carillon concert if you are visiting Bruges in the summertime. The carilloneur may bring forth sacred music, a Brahms lullaby, or possibly even "Deep in the Heart of Texas."

Time: Morning
Direction: Northwest
Lens: Normal

Though clear skies with fluffy clouds nearly always are welcome, often an old canaled city such as Bruges can be pleasing in soft light. So much of the picture is of detailed walls, arches, bridges, and so forth that harsh lighting would not seem in keeping with the mellow colors and textures.

Windmill / Amsterdam, Holland

JACOB VAN RUISDAEL (1628–1682), A FAMOUS DUTCH ARTIST who was also a physician, painted "The Mill," a scene similar to this photograph which was taken near Amsterdam. Two hundred years later in the period of romanticism, his work was widely copied by other artists. In this twentieth century, van Ruisdael's subject matter still intrigues not only photographers, for all the world loves a windmill wherever it may be found.

A Dutch windmill evokes memories of tulips, chocolate, canals, dikes and polders. The windmills of Holland, "more's the pity," are going the way of the passenger pigeon into extinction. The Kingdom of the Netherlands (Low Countries) is just about one-third the size of the state of Virginia, yet at one time it had more than 900 working windmills. Primarily these were used to pump water from their lands lying below sea level behind the dikes. Later some of them were utilized for milling. Although Holland is relatively one of the most thickly populated areas of the world, these peaceful people are not striving to expand beyond their own borders. New land is being built for farms by constructing polders, land reclaimed from the sea.

Waterwheels were known before windmills. The idea of windmills may have been suggested by ships powered by the wind pushing sails. But nothing is original. The derivation of the windmill may have been from the large wind-driven prayer wheels used by Tibetan Buddhists to waft their prayers to their deities more speedily and with less effort than the hand swiveled prayer cylinders required — an early labor-saving device.

In the ancient world the working windmill was unknown. The great desert areas of Persia cried for irrigation. In Seistan, Eastern Persia — hot, dry, dusty — high winds from June to September reach a velocity of 70 miles an hour. Here was the perfect area for the genesis of the windmill in the tenth century.

Every traveler has seen windmills throughout the world — and of all types. The romance attached to windmills is an enigma. Windmills with canvas sails such as those of the Greek Islands and Portugal are more picturesque than the tall, bleak functional ones on the farms of the United States. While most windmills are built high to catch the wind, along the seacoast of Lebanon are hundreds of squat windmills, barely off the ground, which whirl madly, pumping seawater into the many salt vats along the shore.

Windmills became common in Europe in the thirteenth century and were built with towers of stone or brick, rather than of timbers. Holland made a great advance in construction in 1430 with the introduction of the hollow-post mill. The average power of the windmill was 5 to 10 horsepower. It is hardly surprising that with the progress of steam, electric and atomic power our romantic windmills throughout the world are being liquidated.

Time: Late afternoon
Lens: Normal
Direction: Eastward

This is an instance where scouting for an exact camera position during inclement weather finally paid off. Days of overcast had given me very few opportunities during eight days in the area. Two hours before plane time the sky cleared and by car I rushed eight miles to a previously scouted area. In the case of every serious photographer such scouting can be time well spent even if return to the subject is years away, for I have found that to date I've always had to return to a worthwhile subject if I missed it on a previous trip.

Rheinstein Castle / Rhine River, Germany

THE RHINE RIVER WAS THE EASTERN BOUNDARY OF GAUL, but even so, the Romans used the Rhine as a thoroughfare to keep in touch with their Gallic provinces. The vestiges of their towns located on the west bank of the Rhine are today cities such as Cologne, Bonn, Koblenz, Mainz and Strassbourg.

During the Middle Ages, the Germanic tribes who lived east of the Rhine were astute enough to appreciate the strategy of building fortified castles — "watchtowers on the Rhine" — where they could lower the boom on passing vessels and collect tolls. There were some thirty of these pay stations between Mainz and Koblenz during one period.

What happened to these castles and why did they crumble? The obvious answer is greed. These feudal robber barons overplayed their hands. After unsuccessful attempts to unseat these feudal lords who clogged the traffic on the Rhine, Rudolph of Hapsburg, King of Germany, defeated this syndicate of Rhine highwaymen in 1272 and his troops destroyed some of the castles. This did not entirely wipe out the menace and during the Thirty Years War from 1618 to 1648, Swedes, Franch and Spanish all fought for supremacy of the Rhine, and more castles were destroyed in the proceess. In 1689 Louis XIV of France sought control of Alsace-Lorraine and destroyed more castles. The fourth wave decimated the remaining castles on the Rhine during the French Revolution in 1792 when the German armies were forced to retreat beyond the Rhine. Castle walls were razed, their stones used for construction purposes elsewhere and th era of Rhine fortresses ended.

These ancient graystone castles looking like volcanic plugs have shifted from atrophied relics to cultural history today. The Association for Preservation of German Castles, created in 1899, began the restoration of the Rhine castles. Wealthy individuals purchased and rebuilt some of them and Prussian royalty assisted in this revival. Early in the nineteenth century Prince Frederich of Prussia had Rheinstein Castle renovated and added some Gothic features to it.

Two hundred and sixty feet above Father Rhine, near Trechingshausen, Rheinstein Castle is among the most impressive of these restored totems immortalizing the pirate river barons. It still belongs to a Prussian Princess, the Duchess of Mecklenburg, and tourists may visit its museum and restaurant.

These castles are much more opulent now than when they were constructed as family fortresses, built for protection against intruders and from which to do battle if necessary. They are now used as hotels, inns, restaurants and museums. One of them, Castle Katz, is a boys boarding school. From its turreted schoolrooms there is a view of the high cliff where Lorelei, the legendary siren of the Rhine, enticed lonely seamen with her echoing voice. One can imagine a contingent of boarding-school boys singing their Alma Mater, "Hail Castle Katz," to compete with the wails of this nymph of the rock, Lorelei.

A pleasant boat trip on the Rhine gives you some comprehension of the plethora of castles along this *wasserbahn*. On the terraced hillsides above the river many vineyards yield grapes which produce the superb white Rhine wines of Germany.

Time: Morning
Direction: West
Lens: Medium

There is good light all morning until 11:30. Canal traffic diminishes sharply by noon Saturday for the weekend. Several vantage points are along a path above the castle. Dark foliage requires added exposure.

Rothenburg / Germany

IT IS LIKE LIFTING THE LID OF AN OLD FAMILY TRUNK FULL of heirlooms to come upon a town which still has an original medieval appearance and atmosphere, namely, Rothenburg on the Tauber River. You can plan your own Romantic Road through Bavaria to include this town of gabled stone and half-timber houses, a Rathaus (townhall), churches, convents, inns and shops. Many of its five-storied buildings are seen above the mellow walls which surround the town. Can it be that these walls have survived, held together as they are by medieval mortar made of chalk, sand, egg white and cottage cheese?

About the complicated historical background, suffice it to say that Rothenburg reached its zenith between 1350 and 1408 under its great Burgermeister Toppler. It was an Imperial city until 1830 when it was annexed to Bavaria.

Ray Manley has chosen to enter Rothenburg through the Roedergate, a sturdy stone archway flanked by the two houses of gatekeepers and behind which squarely stands the gate tower. Ambling over its narrow cobblestone streets where geraniums overflow the flowerboxes, pleasant odors intrigue you — fresh bread, pastries, coffee, fine wine and food delicacies. You have only to look up to find the source of each one. For the insignia or coat of arms of each tradesman hangs over his doorway identifying his merchandise. No blatant billboards here. Throughout old European towns the bakery and barbershop are universally indicated by the pretzel and the bloodletter's plate.

Attractive, neat windows of the butcher, the apotek, the shoemaker, linen, toy and musical instrument shops also lure you. You quickly become more than a window shopper. We bought a Melodica for sheer fun and learned to finger familiar tunes on its keyboard as we tooted our way through Bavaria driving under the open sky.

Why so many public fountains in Rothenburg? Under threat of medieval sieges, water, of course, was the prime concern of existence. Only the water master knew the secret system of pipes which supplied the town from springs outside the city walls. Death was the penalty if the water master "ratted" and disclosed this information.

Bell towers and a clock tower indicate the "drinking hall" on the Marktplatz in which only patricians could imbibe during the Middle Ages. Nearby is an exhibit of old standards of weights and measures. Foreign merchants were required to pass inspection before being given a permit to sell their merchandise — conscience was still in vogue. A rod had to equal three years' growth of a young willow tree, 16.5 feet.

Bread, the staff of life, was sold by weight at the Brodhaus and woe to the baker whose scales cheated the buyer! On the outside of Rothenburg's walls is a wooden roller. A rope attached to the Baker's Chair ran over this roller and was controlled from the window above it. Lashed into this contrivance, a miscreant baker was lowered into the moat below and dunked as proper punishment for his crime. St. Jacobskirche within the walls was an asylum for condemned criminals. If they could reach this haven they were freed and with a clean slate invited to leave the town.

Time: Morning
Direction: Westward
Lens: Medium and wide angle

Numerous photogenic buildings, walls, and entrances exist here. The east gateway is probably the most interesting. Sign posts and tour buses offer some obstacles, and a stalled car in the narrow road can hold up traffic until the clouds have disappeared.

Neuschwanstein Castle / Bavaria, Southern Germany

NEUSCHWANSTEIN CASTLE IS ONE OF THREE LAVISH PALACES built by Ludwig II of the Wittlesbach family — King of Bavaria from 1864 to 1886.

With its many turrets — round, square, octagonal, rectangular — its circular staircases, great halls, stained glass windows and elegant furnishings, it embodies all the features of a legendary castle. Begun in 1869, it was finally completed seventeen years later.

Ludwig II, because of his personal egotism, psychological peculiarities and his complete withdrawal from the world, has been labeled The Mad King, a Royal Recluse and Misanthrope.

However, were it not for his protective and affectionate patronage of Richard Wagner, the great German composer who was destitute, scorned and rejected, the world might have lost a great composer. The sagas behind the great Wagnerian operas have been incorporated in the frescoes and paintings which cover the walls of Neuschwanstein Castle.

Ludwig II bankrupted his small country with his wild extravagances and his passion for building magnificent palaces for himself. He was unloved by his people and died a tragic death by drowning. But he left to the world three rare palaces, Neuschwanstein, Herrenchiemsee and Linderhof, incomparable examples of the age of castles and kings in Europe. The most romantic and spectacular of these three is Neuschwanstein near Füssen, Bavaria, southern Germany.

Time: Early morning
Direction: Southwest
Lens: Medium

This is a favorite subject, challenging and colorful. Because this beautiful castle lies in the heart of the Bavarian Alps, its weather varies and heavy fog, mist and even a downpour have been experienced. The camera position is across a gorge northeast of the castle gate, reached by a long, roundabout walk and a climb up the opposite hillside. Sunshine strikes the castle no earlier than about 8:30 A.M. in summer due to high mountains to the east. By 11:00 A.M. the sun has moved around to the left, no longer hitting the front. Several other photographs can be made of sides and back of the castle from accessible spots. Yet the effort required to reach this particular vantage point is most rewarding.

LINDERHOF CASTLE NEAR OBERAMMERGAU, BAVARIA, REPRE-sents one of the chaotic dreams of King Ludwig II to "out-French" the French in this small chateau patterned after the Petit Trianon built by Louis XV. Ludwig admired the Bourbons.

This tall young King Ludwig with delicate features and dark, curly hair became monarch of Bavaria at the age of nineteen. He first remodeled the Palace in Munich. Five years later in 1869 he began the construction of Neuschwanstein Castle, the completion of which took seventeen years. During its construction, Ludwig also began the building of Linderhof Castle, not too far from Neuschwanstein, in this enchanting setting against a wooded hillside. Linderhof was completed in a span of five years, with numerous gardens, terraces, pools and outbuildings. There was a Moorish kiosk purchased from France, a theatre setting for Wagnerian operas and a bizarre grotto, the Grotto of Venus, now called the Blue Grotto.

Linder was not a royal name, but that of a farming family from which the King's father had purchased this land. Ludwig retained the name, calling his castle Linderhof.

Nowhere else in the world have we seen such a frenzied extravagance of detailed craftsmanship in porcelain, glass, mirrors, gilt, wood carving, sculpturing, painting, mother-of-pearl and semiprecious stones in one tiny castle. It is a microcosm of architecture, materials and craftsmanship from countries around the world. The sculptured figure of Atlas shouldering the world which crowns the façade of the miniature chateau may epitomize this idea.

Fountains, it is believed, developed from a myth about a wood nymph who was turned into a fountain to escape the pursuit of a river god as she was bathing in his river. The beautiful fountain in the pool at the entrance of Linderhof Castle displays itself like the tail of a snowy egret at the mating season.

Completing Ludwig's triad of fabulous castles, Herrenchiemsee was started in 1878 but was never completed during his lifetime. This also was a French copy — of Versailles, built by Louis XIV. Herrenchiemsee makes Versailles look drab by comparison.

Ludwig was enamored of the beauty and charm of his own cousin, Princess Sophie — who even resembled him to a degree — and became engaged to her. She was the younger sister of Empress Elizabeth, wife of Franz Joseph of Austria. Elaborate preparations for the royal wedding in Munich were completed even to the Golden Coach and the perfectly matched horses when the "pumpkin cracked." Ludwig reverted to his melancholia and broke the engagement. He never married nor had any special interest in women. His affectionate name for his blood-related fiancee had been Elsa, from Wagner's "Tannhauser," or Elsa-Sophie. He signed his letters to her Heinrich, from Wagner's "Lohengrin."

For this sad unbalanced man, Wagnerian operas, castles and his own personal desires meant more to him than any woman, or, in fact, more than his countrymen who finally dethroned him.

Time: Afternoon
Direction: North
Lens: Normal

Each of the three German castles shown is different in setting, style, and purpose. The great fountain is the attraction of this small castle, which is richly ornamented in a setting of forest green. The fountain is turned on manually each hour of the day for about ten minutes.

Votive Church / Vienna, Austria

EMPEROR FRANZ JOSEF ASCENDED THE AUSTRIAN THRONE IN 1848 at the immature age of eighteen, and ruled for sixty-eight years. Before his death in 1916 he was known as The Grand Old Man of Europe.

In 1853, just a year before he married his beautiful Wittelsbach cousin Elizabeth of Bavaria, he barely escaped the knife of an assassin named Libenyi whose hand was stayed by a Viennese butcher named Ettenreich. In gratitude for the preservation of the Emperor's life, Maximilian, Franz Josef's brother, instigated the building of the Votive Church of Vienna.

The Votive Church with its delicate tapering Gothic spires was built between 1856 and 1879, and is therefore considered modern Gothic. Within the church are some excellent paintings, and kaleidoscopic light floods through its beautiful stained-glass windows. Although it was damaged during air raids of 1945, it has again been restored to symmetrical beauty.

After the demolition of the ramparts which surrounded Vienna in ancient times and the subsequent building of the Ringstrasse — during the reign of Franz Josef — the Votive Church was built contemporaneously with many new and well-designed buildings in Vienna including the Opera House, the Burg Theatre, the Rathaus and the new university.

Although to the traveler Vienna's traditional background is one of culture and gaiety, we cannot forget that one of the world's greatest and most respected rulers suffered many tragedies during his lifetime here.

Years after Franz Josef's own narrow escape from murder, his son and heir Crown Prince Rudolph died at the age of thirty-one in a suicide pact with his seventeen-year-old mistress. The Emperor's brother, Maximilian, who became Emperor of Mexico under French intervention in 1863, was court-martialled and shot, after a short reign of four years. In 1898 Empress Elizabeth, Franz Josef's beautiful and gallivanting wife, while vacationing in Geneva, Switzerland, was stabbed in the heart by a lunatic anarchist, dying almost immediately. A final crushing blow came to the great Emperor when his nephew, Archduke Franz Ferdinand and his cousin-wife Sophie — who were to succeed Franz Josef and Elizabeth on the throne of Austria-Hungary — were shot at Sarajevo in 1914, the incident which triggered World War I.

As the visitor steps inside the Votive Church identified with the escape from murder of Franz Josef himself, he is aware not only that the Emperor was a great man who bore the burdens of his country but also that he bore them with a heart bruised and broken by his own personal tragedies.

Time: Morning
Direction: South
Lens: Normal

This twin-towered cathedral is interesting from the formal gardens in front. Vienna has many interesting architectural subjects, and of course, the statues commemorating Strauss and other famous musicians. Camera technique is normal with no unusual problems.

Grand Canal / Venice, Italy

IN THE COMPLEX OF ISLANDS CALLED VENEZIA OR VENICE, the Grand Canal is the central water thoroughfare four miles in length, lined with handsome old palaces, homes and hotels. Much of the art of Venice is in its architecture and is displayed in the Gothic, Byzantine and Renaissance façades of its buildings along the Grand Canal. The once more-colorful fronts of porphyry, pink stone and pearl have been bleached by time and are now in soft muted tones with the same original elegance of lacy stone carving. It is astounding that these dwellings built upon wooden pillars sunk 100 feet into the subsoil, have stood upright for so many centuries.

The mammoth Church of Santa della Salute, built in gratitude for deliverance from a plague in 1630, is said to be resting on a million and a half such wooden piles at the mouth of the Grand Canal.

When not in use the Venetian gondolas — looking like Turkish slippers with upturned toes — are tied to wooden hitching posts along the canal, many of which resemble the barber's pole. For centuries the gondolas have been the communication system of Venice, serving as delivery cart for the ice man, the milkman, the fruit and vegetable vendor as well as being used for private vehicles, as ferries and even as hearses and funeral barges. It is lamentable to see the romantic gondolas, after many generations of use, being obliterated by the numerous motorized boats in the canal.

There are many sidewalks along the sides of the smaller canals which crisscross Venice, and four hundred bridges connecting its 120 islands. So, if you choose, you may visit your neighbor on foot.

Historic Venetian glass and lace are still manufactured on the islands of Murano and Burano. Some of the earlier finesse of craftsmanship has been sacrificed on the altar of speed and quantity production.

Despite these changes, pictorial Venice, it would appear, has changed less than any other of the once great maritime city states of Italy.

Time: Morning
Direction: West
Lens: Wide angle

This is one of the typical views of Venice — typical because it has been done many times before. But it is truly a representative picture. If it's your first time, then it's new to you and it will give you much satisfaction. Later, try for something different. For some reason the poles in the water occasionally change color. It was disappointing recently to see the red and yellow ones suddenly painted a dull brown. The greatest amount of gondola activity occurs during midmorning when people are returning to or leaving their hotels.

St. Mark's Cathedral / Venice, Italy

IN THE PIAZZA SAN MARCO A GALAXY OF VENETIANS AND tourists was sharing the excitement of a Sea Carnival. Many colorful flags were flying. Costumed dancing and resonant Italian singing filled the square with gaiety. The horde of pigeons which usually usurps the piazza had been temporarily discommoded by the festivities.

Life in Venice pivots around St. Mark's Square. From the days when these 120 islands were taking shape out of a swamp, and during Venice's maritime career as a city state, this plaza with its Doges (leaders) Palace, its soaring Campanile, its ornate Clock Tower and St. Mark's Cathedral has been the fulcrum of Venice.

St. Mark's Cathedral is as conglomerate as the mass of foreign people who stroll through its plaza. It is a bewildering mixture of architecture and great works of art which have been brought here as spoils of war from many Mediterranean countries.

This basilica is built in the form of a Greek cross. Each one of the four arms is surmounted by a Byzantine dome and a still larger dome rises above the intersection of the arms. Although the main contours of the cathedral's exterior are oriental, there are unrelated features such as niches with marble statues, pinnacles, and Roman arches plus the famous four tons of Greek-sculptured bronze horses riding high on the façade.

The members of this handsome equine foursome — coveted by conquerors — have shed their gilded coats during their travels hither and yon. They were first removed from Alexandria to Rome to grace Trajan's Arch. From there they were transported to Constantinople. Seized as booty during the Fourth Crusade, they were carried to Venice. Napoleon's conscience permitted him to transport them from Venice to Paris to be used on his own triumphal arch. After the collapse of "The Little Corporal," these beautiful bronze stallions were again welcomed back to Venice.

In the subdued light inside of the cathedral there is visible an aggregation of art forms, icons, altar screens, marble columns, mosaics and many treasures brought home by the powerful Venetian maritime fleet. The tessellated floor, which has been slowly sinking for some years, gives the visitor the sensation of walking on a rolling sea.

A delightful and somewhat humorous legend tells that Venice felt a special affinity for St. Mark because he had once been stranded in a Venetian lagoon. Christ's words of comfort to the disciple had been used as the motto of Venice. Two astute and devious merchants of Venice who traded in Alexandria were given orders to abduct the remains of the evangelist from Egypt and to bring them to Venice. With cunning chicanery they packed this relic, which was sacred to the Venetians, in pickled pork. The Moslems, to whom even the smell of pork is anathema, unwittingly assisted in the process of smuggling the corpse of St. Mark out of Egypt. When it arrived in Venice the construction of the Cathedral of St. Mark was begun in 829 A.D.

Time: Late afternoon
Direction: East
Lens: Wide angle

Crowded St. Mark's Square challenges the photographer to minimize the tourists who are almost always present. Use of shadows from nearby buildings can be effective, directing interest to the colorful front of this famous cathedral. Exposure is normal with fairly fast shutter speed.

Ponte Vecchio / Florence

EUROPE, MORE THAN ANY OTHER CONTINENT, HAS THE CULture of age and the grace of maturity in our opinion.

The Ponte Vecchio (Old Bridge) which spans the Arno River interlinks the art and culture of Florence (Firenze) with the wealth and power which produced it. On one side of the Arno is the residence of the powerful Medici family, Pitti Palace. On the opposite bank of the river they erected their office building, Uffizi Palace, the business and governmental headquarters of the Medicis. Both of these palaces are rare art galleries today with collections of the world's finest art.

An enclosed gallery through the Ponte Vecchio was the route to work of the Medici Grand Dukes who first traded in wool (Florentine wools were famous) and then became international bankers. Ponte Vecchio, built when Florence was a Roman colony, was rebuilt in 1345. For many years the road across the bridge was lined with butcher shops. Cosimo de Medici, lover of arts and the first of his family to use his personal wealth to promote them, had this bloody mess removed from the bridge. For centuries now silversmiths, goldsmiths, small jewelry shops and other small crafts have occupied the shops which crowd the Ponte Vecchio from shore to shore.

In November 1966 the overburdened watershed above the Arno ruptured the dam which controlled the river. Water and mud — one ton for every inhabitant in Florence — were spewed into this ancient and noble city, and cries of anguish arose from millions around the world who know and love Firenze.

Three times previously the Arno had risen above the arches of the bridge. The last great flood had occurred several generations ago in 1844. The bridge was also repaired after World War II when, fortunately, it escaped total demolition.

Would the Ponte Vecchio stand? This time the rampaging river battered the bridge with huge uprooted trees, steel barrels, timbers and unspeakable detritus. Ponte Vecchio quivered but withstood the onslaught. However, the shops were afloat and many of them were swept away.

But today, cleaned and restored, painted a pristine pink, the Ponte Vecchio is in business again and from many viewpoints is one of the most remarkable works of art in Florence.

Time: Late afternoon
Direction: Northeast
Lens: Normal

There are no difficult exposure problems involved, but finding a suitable viewpoint is a bit difficult. Since the 1966 flood new buildings have been built along the Arno River — some offering new views. The bridge has been scaffolded, replastered and repainted. Its structural appearance has been unharmed, but it will be years before the peeling paint and soft colors once more give it the charm of the past.

Forum Romanum (The Roman Forum) / Rome, Italy

AS TIME MOVES FORWARD IT LEAVES ITS FOOTPRINTS INTO which history steps. A partial history of the Roman Forum is left to us in its excavated and restored ruins.

The Forum Romanum was built in a flat swampy area in the lowland between the Capitoline and Palatine hills. Similar to the Greek Agora, it was a city center, a rectangular plaza which housed shops, markets, public buildings and temples. Here the social, religious, commercial and political life centered. During the times of the Caesars five different emperors built a series of forums which adjoined the Roman Forum itself. These powerful and wealthy Caesars modestly built these additional forums to immortalize themselves in masonry and stone. Julius Caesar built the first, Trajan the last. Trajan's monument to himself is considered the finest, its thirty-six Corinthian columns emulating Greek architecture and design.

In this rare photograph, with the backstage floodlighted by the sun, you can almost fancy the wraiths of the old Roman Patricians in their togas, followed by their slaves, moving about in the shadows of the foreground.

Time: Late evening
Direction: East
Lens: Slight wide angle

If I were to choose a favorite result from all my photographs of one of the world's man-made monuments, I would have to choose this one. Though circumstances were responsible for the results, the technique was the same as that in a later view in Monument Valley, Arizona. A single spotlight of warm sunlight and the soft light of low clouds offer to the prepared photographer a few seconds to achieve rewarding results. Three evenings' waiting for such an opening is time well spent, for if you have a feel for your work this reward is a great thrill. You might wait longer and not get the picture, yet for having tried often, an occasional success is most gratifying. Bracketed exposure based on brightest reading and a continued awareness of light change are necessary.

The Colosseum or Flavian Amphitheatre / Rome

TITUS FLAVIUS VESPASIAN, OF PLEBEIAN BIRTH YET EMPEROR of Rome from 70 to 79 A.D., was known as Vespasian. His sons Titus and Domitian followed in succession, but with the murder of Domitian in 96 A.D. this Flavian dynasty ended. Vespasian initiated the building of the incomparable Flavian amphitheatre that is called the Colosseum because of its colossal size. By choosing the old site of Nero's lake close to his infamous Golden House on which to build it, Vespasian hoped possibly to remove the stigma of Nero and at the same time ingratiate himself with his public.

This imperial stone structure is a huge shell of ruins today. Partially destroyed by fire, earthquake and human vandalism, stripped of its travertine coating and the marble within, it is still an awesome sight.

If we had been airborne and hovering over this elliptical arena in 80 A.D. during its dedication by the son of Vespasian (the festivities lasted three months), we would have been incredulous at the scene our eyes beheld. Fifty thousand Romans, in terraced seats encircling the amphitheatre from top to bottom, were seated in inverse ratio to their social and economic status. On the highest level a space was allotted to the harlots. Below them were the plebeians, next, the patricians and the wealthy, while on the lowest level, nobility and the V.I.P.'s sat behind fifteen-foot walls as a protection from the dangers of the arena. Each had surrendered his clay ticket with his seat number thereon for his admission to the performance. Sand — the latin word for sand is *arena* — covered the floor of the amphitheatre where bloody gladiators fought wild animals for the sadistic enjoyment of the multitude above them. Christians were sacrificed ruthlessly to hungry beasts. Sometimes the arena was converted into a shallow lake where sham naval battles were enacted. A vast awning was stretched over the spectators to shield them.

The Romans, following the Greek civilization, copied much Greek art, architecture and sculpture. Here in the Colosseum are found the typical Greek columns — Doric, Ionic and Corinthian. The Greek Theatre, part and parcel of their culture, was a half circle of seats, often on a hillside, with the stage and orchestra below and in front of the audience. The amphitheatre, however, originated in Italy — a double theatre oval in shape and encircled by walls, the stage being the arena in the center.

There are numerous great outdoor amphitheatres in the world today with seating capacities many times that of the Colosseum, but this Flavian Amphitheatre of Rome is as yet unsurpassed in history and fame.

Time: Afternoon
Direction: East
Lens: Normal

Like the Arch of Triumph and the Eiffel Tower, what can you do differently in photographing a popular subject such as the Colosseum? My attitude is that it is new to each person that sees it in person for the first time. It is a great subject under normal conditions, and it's interesting at night when a time exposure will give motion to its activity. Others will photograph it out of focus, distort it, use filters, and so forth. Yet there is still much to be said for a natural interpretation.

Amalfi / Italy

AMALFI MEANS JUST ONE THING TO MOST OF US, THE AMALFI Drive, that ophidian road winding along the shoreline of the blue Mediterranean at the edge of precipitous cliffs.

This blue sea was the foundation of Amalfi's existence and growth in the tenth century when it became a powerful maritime republic — its location on the Gulf of Salerno was strategic. Its name apparently refers to a captain in Emperor Constantine's army, one Amalfo Romano. But its ensign flying high above the town recapitulates its past — a blue background on which is imposed the Maltese Cross and a winged compass.

When the galleys of Amalfi roamed the Mediterranean during the days of the Crusades, the Amalfians founded hospitals in the Levant. From this arose the order of Hospitallers, or the Knights of St. John, in that area. Later, when headquarters of this order were moved to the island of Malta, the Maltese Cross was used as their insignia.

Amalfi also takes credit for the man Flavio Gioia who either invented or improved the magnetic compass in the tenth century A.D. The effects of this compass were far-reaching, as was the code of maritime laws for the Mediterranean which the Amalfians produced. This code governing the traffic of the Mediterranean was recognized as authoritative until 1570 A.D. With such prestige and power, Amalfi even coined its own money.

Off the beaten track of Amalfi Drive, in the town, the black-and-white-façaded stone cathedral of St. Andrews is seen.

The bones of the Apostle St. Andrew are said to be buried in its crypt. Nearby is an imposing campanile. There is scarcely a town in Italy without its beloved bell tower — its campanile.

The Cappuccini Convent of Amalfi has an impressive history going back to 1212 A.D. It passed through the hands of two religious orders before it came into the possession of the Capuchin Monks who held it for 280 years. It hangs precariously on a cliff at the edge of the sea, and a piece of the monastery slid into the Mediterranean in 1899! The Convent, now a hotel under private ownership, has retained much of the monastic atmosphere, including the cloister and loggias draped with bougainvillea, roses and tropical vines.

This is a perfect spot to stop and consolidate your travel gains.

Time: Midmorning
Direction: Eastward
Lens: Wide angle

Like the Greek Island villages, Amalfi is mostly white, yet this emphasizes color. How fortunate is the photographer who finds an occasional foreground that can be used that will not reduce the importance of the main subject. Bougainvillea, my favorite plant, goes well with Amalfi's climate, its peaceful and beautiful setting. I can truly say this was one of my most enjoyable days. The air, normally hazy, had been cleaned by an evening shower and everything worked together for an easy covering of a most photogenic area. Exposure is slightly difficult for backlighting since dark and light subjects are involved. Reading a nearby light-colored stone wall will give a basis for exposure.

Amalfi Night Festival / Italy

FROM THE FLOWERED TERRACE OF HOTEL CAPPUCCINI THERE was a superior view of the spine-tingling fireworks which celebrated a sea festival at Amalfi. As these "bombs burst in air" three destroyers anchored offshore stood out upon the dark sea like ominous toy ships. A Navy band with martial music added to the excitement of that unforgettable evening.

We often forget that Italy, as such, has only been a unified nation for about 100 years. Victor Emanuel II became its first King in 1861. When Italy became a Republic in 1945 only three monarchs had reigned. Previously, Italy's independent city states such as Milan, Venice, Pisa and Florence had constantly fought for maritime supremacy. Pisa subdued the maritime importance of Amalfi around 1135 A.D. and Amalfi declined in stature and population. But it has increased in popularity. Its beaches and cerulean blue waters attract hundreds of visitors each year.

Time: Night
Direction: North
Lens: Normal

I must admit this picture was a welcome bonus. But upon two occasions previously, I witnessed similar seafaring celebrations. The hotel manager was happy to inform his guests of the evening events. Though the fireworks were not scheduled until 11 o'clock that evening, a first exposure was made after sundown, when only a small amount of light remained, to record a slight outline of the coastline. This exposure is two full stops less than the meter reading indicated. Hours later, the fireworks can be recorded with a time exposure at the same time that village lights reflect across the water. The camera, of course, has not been moved during the evening. One of the penalties of being a camera enthusiast is the occasional late dinner caused by frequent evening photographic happenings — many of which can be memorable pictures, more lasting than some of the rather monotonous tour dinners.

Monte Bianco / Courmayeur, Italy

SEEN FROM COURMAYEUR, ITALY, MONTE BIANCO IS PART OF a massive wall of the western Alps called the Mt. Blanc massif. Mt. Blanc, the highest peak in Europe (about 15,700 feet high), lies within France, but France has no monopoly on its beauty. A tripartite, Mt. Blanc massif overlaps the borders of Italy, France and Switzerland. Above 8000 feet there is always some snow and ice, even in the summertime.

In the seventeenth century, visitors merely looked upon Monte Bianco with awe. When scientists began to show a lively interest in this white tower, a doctor living in Chamonix at the base of Mt. Blanc in France made the first ascent to its summit in 1786. Many have scaled it since that time, and mountain climbers and skiers come to the little resort town of Courmayeur in Italy to stay, using it as a base for their holiday activities on the slopes of Monte Bianco.

Those of us who are not mountain goats can have the chilling thrill of reaching the Pass of the Giants 11,000 feet high at the base of the Italian peak called Dente del Giante. Having ascended to this point by cable car, we can then transfer to another aerial tramway and swing across an ice-clad valley to Aiguille du Midi in France. The final section of this aerial trip returns you to mundane earth, the base of Mt. Blanc in Chamonix, France.

The Alps are not a wide range of mountains so it is quite possible to go up and over, or down and under them. In 1786 a Frenchman suggested building a tunnel under this massif to connect Italy and France. He was considered a wild-eyed Jules Verne of his time. Less than two hundred years later, in 1958, construction of just such a tunnel was begun and within six and a half years it was completed and opened for traffic. Six hundred vehicles an hour can traverse this seven-mile tunnel. For emergencies there are turnouts or lay-bys.

As for us, we prefer to go the Olympian route up and over where for a short time we may feel the ecstasy of heights and a possible rapport with the old mythological gods of the mountains.

Time: Morning
Direction: Westward
Lens: Normal

Europe's highest mountain differs greatly on the Italian side from its appearance on the western or French side. Huge rock formations hide the tallest peak and it is with some difficulty that one finds a viewpoint free of these lesser peaks. Haze can be a problem here. A Polaroid filter can help if the haze is not too bad. Backlighting emphasizes the haze problem. A meter reading can be erroneous if one reads on the reflection of the snow and clouds. Cable car vantage points have made it easier to view Monte Bianco from nearby mountains — a great advantage to the photographer.

Zermatt and the Matterhorn / Switzerland

THE NAME MATTER IS PREEMINENT IN THIS REGION OF SWITzerland where the alpine town of Zermatt lies at the head of the Visp Valley on the Matter River and at the foot of the 14,870-foot peak, the Matterhorn. The great mountain bestrides the border of Italy and Switzerland but the town of Zermatt is wholly Swiss, from its rock-roofed chalets to its belled animals meandering through its streets.

Zermatt is a rendezvous of mountain climbers. Many men and women with sturdy frames and bulging calves, clad in alpine clothes and carrying their packs and alpine stocks, plod up the mountain slopes in the early morning and return wearily and happily in the late afternoon. The village is charming. Its hotels, pensions, restaurants and shops are fringed with geraniums. In true Swiss manner everything is neat and attractive. Even the doctor's macabre sign "Sports Accidents" seems snug and comforting.

Those who are not alpine climbers may still have the thrill of reaching the base of the Matterhorn by *seilbahn,* cable car. From the town of Zermatt the lofty Matterhorn — unless curtained with clouds — seems to float like a solidified mirage in the sky.

Time: Early morning
Direction: West
Lens: Normal

This is possibly the most photogenic village-mountain combination anywhere. Should one arrive in Zermatt in the rain and have to wait a day or two or longer and at last at sunrise look to the west and see this magnificent peak mantled in fresh snow, then he too would feel this is the greatest thrill in scenic photography. There are countless foreground possibilities. Generally speaking, light is better in the morning.

Jungfrau / Wengen, Switzerland

HOW MUCH MORE SATISFYING IT WOULD BE IF WE COULD interpret our emotional responses to the world's magnificent sights in some fashion other than mere words!

The Jungfrau is a high, white, pyramidal mountain mass in the Bernese Oberland Alps of Switzerland. This lofty maiden (*Jungfrau* = young lady) in her Shangri-la never appears to grow any older. Her visage is ageless.

Never have we seen an unattractive or unlovely Swiss town even when it was burdened with tourists. From the neat and refreshing town of Interlaken, we have a preview of the Jungfrau. Not far from Interlaken in the Lauterbrunnen Valley we can see this changeless virgin through a foreground of a long trough-like green valley where sparkling waterfalls from melting glaciers drop from heights. Clear rushing streams flow through Lauterbrunnen like sinuous silver bands. Such a quantity of waterpower provides electricity for many purposes in the Bernese Oberland Alps.

Wengen, at an altitude of about 4000 feet, lies on the cheek of the valley and is an old Swiss town. Its rare beauty and location have been discovered and now it is also a resort town. At various seasons of the year we have seen these mountainsides carpeted with edelweiss and large low clumps of "alpine roses," white and pink.

Skiers, mountain climbers and less exotic sightseers board an electric narrow-gauge railway train which moves from Scheidegg up the steep side of this mountain mass. En route it runs for 4¾ miles through a tunnel under Mt. Eiger and the Mönch and suddenly we find ourselves at the top of the world, 11,000 feet high, at Jungfraujoch — the saddle or the yoke. We feel as though with closed eyes we might reach out and touch the peak itself.

The summit was first reached in 1811 by the Meyers brothers. This was the breakthrough, and since then many others have successfully scaled this lofty peak. The real birth of mountaineering took place in Switzerland and the English, as a group, seem to have been the first people who started mountaineering for fun.

Occasionally the Jungfrau hides her features under her own brand of face powder called *bise* — in reality a cold blast of northeast wind which whips a veil of snow and ice over her nose.

Time: Afternoon
Direction: South
Lens: Medium

This is one of the natural beauty spots of the world, and probably the most accessible mountain, with numerous vantage places. Yet, weather can be temperamental — overcast, rainy, foggy or hazy. I once waited five days without even seeing the mountain. Except for the longest days of the year, because this mountain faces north the best light is afternoon until sunset when the snow turns pink or salmon red. Care must be taken not to underexpose due to brilliant light reading as the detail of the hanging glacier is important and might be lost.

Tossa De Mar/Costa Brava, Spain

THE BEAUTY OF THE BEACH AT TOSSA DE MAR ON THE COSTA Brava is to be enjoyed only in the morning hours when the plague of humans which swarms over it and usurps it all afternoon is still sleeping or tending blistered, sunburned integuments. During the morning local fishermen mend their nets on the beach and put out to sea for the day's catch to sell to the tourists.

This Mediterranean beach on the Costa Brava has lured masses of visitors. Inexpensive, all-inclusive tours, predominantly English and German, come by busloads to Tossa de Mar. If a stranger is able to find a two-by-five foot space into which he can cram his torso on the beach, he is apt to hear a lilting cockney on the right of him and a gutteral German on the left.

The sight is reminiscent of the congealed mass of suety flesh covering the stone beaches of Yalta in midsummer. Cheap trade demands cheap housing, and flimsy cottages for tourists have sprung up like morning toadstools at Tossa de Mar. The ragged, rugged coast of Spain stretching from Barcelona to the French border, known as Costa Brava, can be best enjoyed from a small boat on the blue Mediterranean at arm's length from the shore. From here the fishing villages and beaches are picturesque. BOOMING is the adjective most fitted to Tossa de Mar at the moment.

Time: Morning
Direction: Southward
Lens: Normal

The Costa Brava is a pleasant surprise in that its beaches are fully equal to those of France and Italy. Because the beach is shared by both fishermen and sunbathers a variety of pictures is available. After the beaches have been cleared of drying nets, sun worshipers add even more color. I am sure most photographers are aware of the seashore's brilliant reflective light.

Avila / Spain

WALLED CITIES REFLECT A BASIC INSTINCT IN MAN — SELF-preservation. Today, when a group of atoms could destroy the world, a walled city such as Ávila is no more than an anachronism, an historical relic. This ponderous cordon of gray granite is still intact and our admiration and curiosity drive us to know more about it.

Ávila was built in a strategic pass where it could control the traffic into New Castile. Romans, Visigoths, Moors and Christians all possessed it in sequence. The Moors and Christians shuttled back and forth conquering and reconquering this city. Ávila in its time was a thriving city behind the walls. Although they are only a little more than a mile and a half in length, they completely surround the city and an incredible number of fortified towers (some eighty-six of them) built into the walls gave extra protection. In view of the excess of battlements, it is surprising to find nine gateways to the city, for these would also need safeguarding.

The fall of the Roman Empire and the departure of its legions, which had protected the Roman colonies in Spain, gave rise to the building of walled cities. The former open cities became prey for the barbarians, so walls were built around towns while castles were protected by walls and moats. The walls of Ávila were built so high that only the towers of the Cathedral can be seen above them from the surrounding ramparts. These great walls were restored in 1090 A.D.

During the Spanish Inquisition when the Moriscos and Marranos (converted Moors and Jews) were driven out of Ávila by the Catholic monarchs, Ávila fell into decline. Today it is a quiet walled city proceeding on its customary way of day-to-day living. It has a Plaza Mayor (Main Square), a market, churches and a cathedral and along its cobblestone streets live its people. There is a touch of its colorful antiquity still seen in the burros and carts which bring produce to the *mercado*. Pilgrims come to Ávila to the tomb of its patron, Saint Teresa, who was born here and whose shrine is here.

The son and heir to the throne of Isabella and Ferdinand was educated in the University in Ávila and when this young man died he was buried in a monastery not far from the walls of Ávila.

Other than Carcassone in southern France, there is probably no walled city in such an excellent state of preservation as Ávila. These two walled cities give us a glimpse of the fear and courage of men of the Middle Ages.

Time: Morning
Direction: West
Lens: Normal

On two days during the month people gather to trade and sell livestock. Because cars, trucks and crowds are involved, a small section of this great walled city must be chosen to photograph during this time. A day or so later all will be normal once more, and general views again available. I have found that having to overcome unexpected obstacles often results in a better picture.

Alcazar / Segovia, Spain

IT WOULD HAVE BEEN A COLORFUL EXPERIENCE IN AN EX-
tremely dramatic setting to have been a guest at the coronation
of Isabella in this Alcazar (palace) in Segovia, Spain, in 1474.
She came to the throne succeeding her brother, Henry IV, and
was crowned Queen of the Independent Kingdom of Castile.

Castile occupied much of the northern area of Spain. To
the east of it lay the Kingdom of Aragon. Isabella had married
her cousin Ferdinand V, King of Aragon, in 1469, so shortly
after her ascendency to the throne of Castile, these two important
independent kingdoms were united under King Ferdinand and
Queen Isabella. This kingdom then became the core to which
other independent kingdoms of Spain were later attached, culmi-
nating in the unified country of Spain.

The Alcazar of Segovia, about fifty miles north of Madrid,
standy solidly and loftily on a rocky projection of land. It seems
to belong to some fairytale and appears invincible. For many
years it was used as a royal palace but it presently houses a
museum containing documents pertaining to Spanish history.

There are some 1400 castles in Spain, many of them ancient
and crumbling, but Segovia's stands erect with head high, sym-
bolyzing a by-gone day.

Having driven out most of the Moors who had occupied
Spain for 700 years, this same Queen Isabella in 1492 finally
uprooted the last of the Moors from Andalucia (southern Spain)
and took over their last stronghold, the Alcazar of Granada
called the Alhambra.

Holding court in this elegant and elaborate Moorish palace,
quite unlike the stark Castilian Alcazar of Segovia, Isabella
received Christopher Columbus and, prodded by her royal
treasurer to invest in this adventure, financed the visionary
Columbus who was seeking a short route to the Indies.

This year of 1492 was an eventful one for Spain. She had
rid herself of the Moors and had laid claim to a vast territory
in the New World.

Time: Afternoon
Direction: East
Lens: Normal

*The castle that has symbolized Spanish castles is just a morning's drive from
Madrid. During our visit the weather improved each day, and original pictures
we made were discarded for those of progressive clouds, etc. Two telephone
wires do offer some obstacle, though by now the bright copper has probably
oxidized and is less noticeable. The stream beneath the castle offers additional
foreground. Remember, however, that the stream is not as pure as it appears.*

Eiffel Tower / Paris

THE NUMBER OF EYES WHICH HAVE LOOKED UP AT OR DOWN from the Eiffel Tower since this steel pylon was erected would be an astronomical figure if it were known.

Eiffel Tower is symbolic of Paris, rising almost 1000 feet into the blue sky over France's capital. It was scornfully called Eiffel's Folly, but in spite of jibes and doubts, Alexandre Auguste Eiffel successfully erected this 7300 tons of steel and iron for the Paris Exhibition of 1889. Its cost, prodigious at that time, was over a million dollars. But this was recouped within the first year of the Exhibition through gate receipts. For many years it outranked in stature all the skyscrapers of the world.

Unless you have a sudden attack of acrophobia, you will undoubtedly ascend by elevator to one of the various galleries located en route to the top. A powerful radio station at the apex of this pinnacle broadcasts time signals to the world. Looking down upon the rushing traffic of Paris, the busy boating on the Seine and the human pygmies scampering about, an earthbound being can get a new outlook on life from this vantage point.

No one ever tells a visitor in Paris, "Don't miss Eiffel Tower!" You wouldn't and you couldn't.

Time: Dusk and night
Direction: East
Lens: Wide angle

Paris' famous landmark has hundreds of possibilities, yet my favorite one is this view from the fountains across the Seine. This is a multiple exposure, similar to those of the Arch of Triumph and Notre Dame. Yet, a few comments concerning timing will help the first-time visitor. During the summer evenings, the water fountains are not turned on until 9:00 in the evening, quite a while after sundown. The camera position should be chosen during daylight hours with a first exposure for the sky just after sundown. With camera on a steady tripod, the camera must be carefully guarded against movement until total darkness or when the lights and water are turned on. At this time, the second exposure of considerable duration can be made. A bit of misty rain gives a glow to the sky — a raindrop on the lens can give a few "ghost" images, apparent in my effort. A lens shade at night is often very necessary for this protection, as well as preventing the damaging effects of oncoming car lights.

Time: Morning
Direction: West
Lens: Normal

Because of the constant movement about the Arc de Triomphe, a shutter speed of 100th of a second or faster is necessary to avoid blur. This side of the arch which faces the Champs-Élysées is a morning photograph.

Arc de Triomphe de L'Étoile / Paris

LIKE THE SPREADING RAYS OF A STAR, A DOZEN STREETS RADI-
ate from the Place de l'Étoile into Paris. In its solid grandeur,
the heroic Arc de Triomphe straddles the center of this star — the
Étoile. Its proportions make it the largest triumphal arch in the
world. The Arc was built as a memorial to the Revolutionary and
Napoleonic triumphs. Begun in 1806, thirty years were required
to complete this arch which is so famous for beauty of architecture and sculpture.

From the Place de la Concorde, one moves up the Champs-
Élysées to meet the Arc de Triomphe face to face. On the other
side of the arch the street becomes the Avenue of la Grande
Armée. Ascending its 162 feet of height one has an overlook of
the nearby area of Paris. Halting beneath the arch itself one
humbly looks down on the Grave of the Unknown Warrior where
a nameless hero of France lies interred, representing her unsung
dead of World War I. Here the perpetual flame burns — the
Flamme du Souvenir — so that the memory of their courage may
never be extinguished.

Time: From 7:00 to 11:00 P.M.
Direction: West
Lens: Normal

*There are a number of hotels and bank buildings facing the arch where a good
vantage point can be found. But my favorite is from the roof of a penthouse on
top of a large advertising agency building. This building, incidentally, was
SHAFE headquarters during World War II. It is necessary to obtain permission
from the building guard and the advertising agency public relations department
to view the arch from the penthouse roof. Tourists will have no difficulty getting
this permission during daytime hours. At night the services of a trusted employee
as well as the guard are necessary — and payment must be made for the time of
both individuals. This is a multiple exposure made similarly to that of the Eiffel
Tower. The technique is basically the same. A simpler nighttime view could be
made from the safety zone in the middle of the Champs-Élysées where one gets
an unobstructed view of the arch.*

Cathedral of Notre Dame de Paris / Paris, France

THERE ARE LITERALLY HUNDREDS OF CATHEDRALS OR churches in the world dedicated to Our Lady — Notre Dame of some place or another. But when one simply says "Notre Dame" there is no question that he is referring to the handsome square-towered edifice, Notre Dame de Paris.

It is by no means the largest or the most elaborate of European cathedrals. It has a relative simplicity which is pleasing. After its construction, begun in the twelfth century, it underwent the despoiling of man and time until the end of the eighteenth century, and was restored in the nineteenth century. At that time the central spire was added to the Cathedral. The Rose or Wheel Window over the entrance is typical of many Gothic cathedrals.

Without doubt, the most poignant historic event held in Notre Dame was the crowning of Napoleon Bonaparte as Emperor of France in 1804. Pope Pius VII, having been persuaded to leave Rome and come to Paris for this affair (which according to hierocratic custom should have taken place in the Pope's own bailiwick), performed the ceremony which made Napoleon France's first Emperor, "anointed of the Lord." However, Napoleon himself, believing in self-service, took the crown from the hands of the Pope and, with Napoleonic aplomb, clamped it securely on his own head.

Time: Night
Direction: East
Lens: Wide angle

From the vantage point of a corner restaurant window, it is possible to photograph Notre Dame's west-facing front by dusk and artificial illumination. This twenty-minute time exposure included the arc lights of a tour boat going up the Seine, and the streaks of parking lights and taillights of cars. During this time an auto overturned near the bridge, yet a few French couples apparently ignored it, as their images recorded with little blur. A meter reading of spotlights on Notre Dame taken the previous evening will indicate the length of the exposure. Car lights and boat spotlights add interest to Paris at night.

Pont du Gard / Nimes, France

THE HALLMARK OF ROMAN ENGINEERING IS APPARENT WHEN you look upon Le Pont du Gard near Nimes, France.

Nimes, a flourishing Roman metropolis of Gaul, needed water for its public baths and its vigorous and thriving city life. As a specially privileged city, independent of the rule of the Roman Gallic pro-consuls of Narbonne, Nimes had a temple to Diana, a great amphitheatre and, in true Roman tradition, city baths. The Romans had always demanded more water than preceding civilizations for personal use. Rome, which had its official Superintendent of Waterworks, was water conscious. Some two hundred cities in the Roman colonies of Spain, North Africa, Syria and France had aqueducts built by the Rmans.

Le Pont du Gard is a distinguished example of fine engineering — strength and grace combined. It was not destroyed by the vandals who ravaged Nimes at the height of its prosperity and at the same time tore up the interlinking channels of the bridge. The purpose of Le Pont du Gard was to bring fresh water to Nimes from Uzès, a city 39 miles distant from the aqueduct.

Agrippa, the Roman General, directed the building of this aqueduct which was begun in 19 B.C. The great building blocks of amber and gray stone were cut from nearby quarries. Three tiers of handsomely proportioned arches form the Pont. Two lower rows of arches are surmounted by a span of thirty-five smaller arches. On top of the upper tier there was a covered water trough, but the roof has vanished today. There was also a second conduit just below the top tier of arches.

Since the days of the Romans a vehicle road has been built across the bridge. Crossing to the left bank of the river, it is easy to follow a footpath through a thicket of trees to the edge of the water and to walk beneath one of these great arches. In such intimacy one appreciates more fully the superb engineering skill of the Romans and their competent building technique in creating this great stone aqueduct. It has withstood heat, cold, rain and storms. It may have shuddered under some of nature's hard onslaughts but it has continued to exist for twenty centuries.

In the early days of summer the Gard River seems a very gentle stream, hardly worthy of this monumental overpass. Seven smaller streams — whose names are all prefixed by the name Gard — combine to form the Gard River in a gorge upstream from Le Pont du Gard. The river then continues to meander toward the Mediterranean, joining the wide Rhone River near Beaucaire.

Time: Afternoon
Direction: East
Lens: Normal

An uncluttered Roman ruin in a fine state of repair and a different subject for variety in one's collection of world photographs — such is Pont du Gard. This handsome aqueduct may be photographed both morning and afternoon as it runs north and south. Usually there are no cars or other foreign objects to mar its beauty.

Le Puy-en-Velay / Auvergne, France

LE PUY-EN-VELAY LIES IN THE BASIN OF AN ANCIENT LAKE where rocky pillars jut upward like blunt fingers.

Perched like an eagle's eyrie on one of these pinnacles in the valley is the Chappelle St. Michel-d'Aiguille. To reach its summit the visitor must climb almost perpendicular stairs laid in the side of this needle-like plug.

A second dramatic *puy* or peak is surmounted by a huge and impassive statue of Notre Dame de France built from the cold metal of guns captured in the Crimean war.

Completing the religious triad is the early Romanesque Cathedral of le Puy where their Notre Dame is a black virgin. The original black virgin brought from Egypt by St. Louis has been replaced by the present one. The Cathedral is an integral part of the old town of le Puy and is built on the edge of the volcanic mass which overlooks the valley and both the ancient and the less-ancient town of le Puy.

Pilgrims including Popes and Kings have come to le Puy and even now the feast of the Assumption in August draws many modern pilgrims to this city.

On a sunny May morning when church bells were ringing, we climbed the cobblestones of Rue des Tables, where no vehicles were permitted, to join the Mass held in the Cathedral. The dark nave, dimly lighted except for bright altar candles, had an air of informality. Most of the worshipers came with heads uncovered and joined joyously in the congregational singing which was in French — not Latin. The Mass was clearly read in comprehensible French.

As we were returning down the cobblestone street, several French women invited us to stop in their sidewalk homes to see their hand-made lace — le Puy Lace. Formerly the lace known as "guipure" was also made here but the factories have now taken over this production.

Although this quiet town of le Puy belongs to history with its feudal days and Crusaders, it is an exciting place to visit because of its background and its uncanny landscape. Put your finger on the city of Lyon, France. Move it southwest beyond St. Etienne and you will find yourself *in absentia* in le Puy.

Time: Morning
Direction: West
Lens: Normal

As a part of France, these chapel-covered volcanic necks only enhance my feeling that France has the greatest variety of scenic attractions of all Europe. After Paris one should spend time in the French countryside. The great number of interesting places could keep a photographer busy for weeks.

Château de Chambord / Loire Valley, France

AFTER YOU HAVE VISITED ALMOST THIRTY CASTLES BUILT BY French royalty one after another along the Loire Valley it seems as though the kings of France had been trying to "outdo the Joneses."

These great stone châteaux along the Loire River and some of its tributaries were built for the kings, their mistresses and wives for pure pleasure.

Francis I who became King at the age of twenty, had a longer list of personal castles to his credit than did the Mad Ludwig of Bavaria. Amboise, where Francis spent his boyhood, Blois, Chambord and Chenonceaux all have his indelible fingerprints on them.

This luxurious mode of living of the French kings of the Renaissance period has left us a string of châteaux which are today national monuments to a glorious past.

Chambord is doubtless the most grandiose of this collection. Francis I, having already lived in two Loire mansions, wished a "house of his own" — a phrase which has a familiar ring even today. Chambord, with all the proper appurtenances anticipated in castle architecture, has turrets, parapets, wings, great halls and royal chambers. It fills the specifications of an ideal château or castle. Claim is made that there are four hundred rooms in Chambord. It you have ever tried to count the rooms in a château you will find that every nook and entryway is counted as a room. No weekend houseparty could feel crowded in this hunting lodge of Francis I.

Of particular interest is a banistered staircase — a pair of circular stairs built to fit into the large tower in the center of the château. These two staircases rise side by side, but since they start from different locations on the main floor, they criss-cross each other as they spiral upward. If only a polished rail had been installed, what a marvelous joyride the guests of Francis I could have had sliding down the banisters on their way to the great banquet hall! When the Chambord court was "at home" in this *château de plaisance,* invited guests would arrive in coaches and carriages attended by coachmen and footmen; horses were changed en route at post stations between Paris and their destination.

Since the luxurious and fashionable life of France centered in these châteaux in the Loire Valley, merchants took up residence nearby to furnish the demands of royalty for their festivals, balls and sporting events.

Satiated with too many castles and with no wag left in us, we found a pleasant *bistro* in a nearby village. Sitting on its small terrace at a table with red-checked linen, we consolidated our gains and rested our feet as we enjoyed a lark pie and sparkling white Monmousseau wine.

Time: Afternoon
Direction: East
Lens: Normal

This is a unique structure well worth photographing either during the afternoon or at evening when it is illuminated. Great gardens and trees offer possible variety in foreground. There is a somewhat commercial atmosphere, yet if one can put himself into the mood of the château's earlier days, it is different than most other châteaus of the Loire Valley.

Tower Bridge / London

A BRIDGE TO MOST OF US IS SIMPLY A CONVENIENT MEANS OF crossing a body of water or an open space. In primitive times vines, ropes and fallen trees served as bridges as they do even today in Nepal and Tibet. The Persians crossed the Hellespont into Greece on pontoon — floating — bridges in 480 B.C. Pontoon bridges are still used today in military operations and emergencies. The permanent bridge has developed with civilization and engineers have designed various types of bridges using many kinds of materials in their construction — wood, stone, iron, brick, concrete and new alloys of steel as well as structural aluminum.

Until 1750 old London Bridge was the only one crossing the Thames River. This looked more like a village than a bridge, completely crowded with houses, shops and even a chapel. Tower Bridge is the easternmost bridge over London's pulsing coronary artery, the Thames River. Its high Gothic towers blend with the architecture of the Tower of London, that grim old fortress, palace and prison next to which it stands. This similarity is not accidental, for Sir John Wolfe Barry, youngest son of the architect for the Gothic Houses of Parliament, obviously incorporated some inherited ideas in the building of Tower Bridge to harmonize it with the nearby Tower of London. Ugly structural steel pylons have been faced with granite and Portland stone to form the handsome gothic towers of this unusual bridge.

Since it is a bascule bridge, the open two-hundred-foot span separates in the middle and each section folds back against its tower like a yawning mouth to permit good-sized ships to pass through it and into the upper end of the Pool of London.

Below the Tower Bridge is the great shipping harbor, the Pool of London. A system of harbors connected by canals provides dockage with great loading facilities for international shipping. This area is heavily protected by the Thames Division of Scotland Yard's vigilant patrol.

Old London Bridge (of nursery rhyme fame) withstood wear and tear for six hundred years before "falling down" at which time it was replaced with a modern London Bridge. It is included in the twenty-five bridges which today cross the tide-controlled Thames between Tower Bridge and Twickenham on the outskirts of London.

Father Thames is still the progenitor of the throbbing life of this enormous, sprawling and still-growing city of London. Floodlighted at night, Tower Bridge and the Tower of London become awesome, ghostly, Gothic giants.

Time: Morning — View from a Helicopter
Direction: Northwest
Lens: Normal

A day with fluffy clouds and a bright blue sky may be unusual and a bit out of tune with one's general impression of "foggy" London town, yet I have pleasantly experienced a few such beautiful days, though more often it is cloudy with some bright periods. The bridge is raised for traffic which is timed to the high tide. This time would be available in the local paper.

Westminster Palace (Houses of Parliament)/London

IF THE HOUSES OF PARLIAMENT AND BIG BEN WERE TO DIS-appear by magic, London would look naked. Even the massive bulk of Buckingham Palace would leave no such gap in London's skyline as would the disappearance of Westminster on the River Thames. Westminster Palace, containing the House of Commons, the House of Lords and the Great Clock Tower, is symbolic of British stability throughout the Commonwealth.

It is normal to wonder why the home of England's Royal Courts, Parliament, should be called a palace, Westminster. Names will stick like burrs and this one has become permanent although irrelevant. Originally this was the Palace of King Canute, the red-faced Dane who conquered England and became King of Norway, Denmark and England in 1016. Fire destroyed the Palace in 1034. In 1840 Sir Charles Barry redesigned Westminster Palace for the use of their law courts, British Parliament. Its "perpendicular Gothic" architecture has a simplicity and beauty which endures.

The clock and chimes of Westminster have a formidable history. After years of political bickering, the Great Clock, ten times larger than a normal cathedral clock, was completed. Another tug of war ensued over the casting of the large bell and the smaller chimes which would strike the hour, the half hour and the quarter hours. Finally, during the tenure of Sir Ben-jamin Hall, First Commissioner of Works, arguments arose in Parliament over a name. Sir Benjamin, a man of great bulk, also of great popularity, was familiarly called Big Ben. He was suggesting the name of St. Stephen when a British wag, hot and weary of much blathering, shouted out, "Why not call it Big Ben and be done with it?" So it was, and so it is!

This may be as apocryphal as the Midnight Ride of Paul Revere but it is infinitely more rational.

The great fourteen-ton bell started duty in 1859. Twice it has tolled the death of English Kings but it has also announced joyous events. The B.B.C. first broadcast the voice of Big Ben at midnight in 1923, ringing in the year of 1924 when crystal sets were the receivers. The first B.B.C. hookup with the British Empire occurred in 1932. Daily now Big Ben sounds throughout the Empire giving the accurate signal of Greenwich Mean Time.

Time: Late evening and after dark
Direction: Northwest
Lens: Normal

When street lights and building lights are turned on about sunset it is simple to wait for an exposure balance that will call for a few seconds time, allowing for a few car, double-decked buses or boat light streaks. When these lights are later than sunset, a preliminary exposure to some blue sky can be made, underexposing a full 100 percent. Later, after darkness, additional exposures can be made at will for accent lighting.

Buckland-in-the-Moor / England

A SHORT HOLIDAY IN BUCKLAND-IN-THE-MOOR IS A PHYSICAL and spiritual emollient after the heat and excitement of a visit to London.

Buckland-in-the-Moor lies on the Dart River upstream from Dartmouth, in the Dartmoor Forest, near Buckfastleigh in the Moorland country, in the province or shire of Devon. This seems a perversity of words but the English understand it perfectly and happily some foreigners find their way to this tranquil area. The nearest sizeable town is Ashburton. Here one finds cob houses (walls made of clay, gravel and straw) with heavily thatched, manicured roofs. Flower gardens and narrow lanes add to the unpressurized atmosphere and one feels that "tomorrow is also a day."

In this area you may leave your car and tramp, hike, saunter or climb to the heather-clad hills. On the top of Buckland Beacon, about one thousand feet above sea level, you will be surprised to find the Ten Commandments carved in the bare rock.

There is a limpid stream on whose banks you may rest in Buckland-in-the-Moor. There is a tiny church you will never forget. From the clock on the church the parishioners read the time of day not from numerals but from twelve letters around its face which spell, MY DEAR MOTHER.

Time: Morning
Direction: Northwest
Lens: Normal

This is a real gem in the English countryside, and to find it with clear weather is so much the better. Brilliant green grass is always of interest to a desert dweller, yet one must remember a lot of rain must fall to produce such grass. Expose for the grass and everything else will fall into place. This is the bonus one finds when searching the unfamiliar areas — just as if you were the first discoverer.

Castle Combe / England

CASTLE COMBE IN THE COTSWOLD HILLS OF SOMERSETSHIRE shows a calm and quaint face to those who visit it. Some call Castle Combe (Castle Valley) a pretty town but "pretty" implies youth and there is nothing young about this gentle, aged village. It was in existence during the Roman occupation of Britain. An old burial ground has produced fragments of a bronze crown and a seal identified as Roman.

The invasion of the Danes in 878 was responsible for the destruction of the old Castle or Castellon on the hill. Its round tower, considered unsafe, was later deliberately destroyed. Castle Combe — in the twelfth century a Barony of the Earl Reginald of Dunstanville — belonged to the family for centuries. Thirty manors were dependent upon it.

In the aisle of Castle Combe's church today you will find a tomb portraying a recumbent knight in armor — said to be the grave of the last Dunstanville.

By 1368 these feudal farms were being "let for money and not for bondage." Nevertheless, strict regulations existed which have a ludicrous ring to our ears today. There was an ominous gallows field, a ducking stool for eavesdroppers and gossipers, stocks and a pillory for lesser offenders. Poachers (including guilty parsons) were fined for hunting deer and rabbits in the park.

Through marriage, Sir John Fastolf became Lord of Castle Combe in which capacity he functioned for fifty years, until his death in 1460. With the welfare of his tenants in mind, he used his wealth to bring prosperity, peace and quiet to Castle Combe. New buildings arose, cottages and mills were built, even a tavern was provided. Use of this town groggery was limited to one day a week and townsmen were exhorted not to play dice.

Shakespeare took the liberty of converting the name of Sir John Fastolf into Falstaff in his *Henry IV*. There is perhaps little in common between the dramatic and historic characters. Although Sir John Fastolf died in 1460 at the age of eighty — before the birth of Shakespeare in 1564 — it is good fun to imagine that the ghosts of Shakespeare's Falstaff may be poltergeisting about you when you visit the Old Manor House in Castle Combe which now welcomes paying guests. At the White Hart Inn and Castle Inn there is an atmosphere of history and antiquity.

The old stone cottages of Castle Combe with their moss-grown stone roofs look much as they did in the feudal days, and there is a delightful air to the old town which is ten miles northeast of Bath and one hundred miles west of London.

Time: Late morning
Direction: Northeast
Lens: Normal

Afternoon light would be just about as good, but this time was chosen because tours and throngs of people arrive just before noon and England's fairest village takes on a less peaceful atmosphere. A good detailed map is required to find this tiny spot near Bath, west of London. Good weather not only aids the photographer, but brings out the sun-loving Englishman. My most helpful advice is to arrive as early as possible. The English are courteous and polite and only too happy to help with your picture, either as models or by their retreat out of sight.

Anne Hathaway's Cottage / Stratford, England

ANNE HATHAWAY'S COTTAGE WHICH SHE LEFT IN 1582 AT the age of twenty-six to marry the eighteen-year-old Will Shakespeare, seems to have intrigued historians more than Anne herself. This was Anne's cottage only in the sense that it was her girlhood home. The twelve-room farmhouse belonged to her father, Richard Hathaway, and was in Shottery, a mile from Stratford. Farm buildings stood nearby the cottage and a hundred acres of land were part of the Hathaway holdings.

The Richard Hathaways were a respected family with an apparently unsullied background of many years. It was, no doubt, a blow to their respectability to find that their daughter Anne was three months pregnant with Will Shakespeare's child. Their marriage was quickly arranged "by special license" with only one posting of the bans. A girl, Susanna (later called Anne) was born in May, 1583.

The young husband provided no little home for his bride but instead, under financial necessity, they lived with Shakespeare's parents in Stratford on Henley Street. Under the threatened penalty for poaching, Shakespeare took off for areas out of reach of the sheriff's arm and finally arrived in London where he spent many years of his life.

The life, extramarital love life, and the deathless literature and drama of this prima donna have undergone fierce debate, loving tolerance, questions of veracity, glorified adulation and still remain conversational conjecture for many. But the story of his wife Anne disappears from the pages of history as she apparently disappeared from Shakespeare's life like a cloud evaporating in slow motion.

In Shakespeare's last will and testament he disposed of his property to his two remaining daughters and grandchildren and more or less as an afterthought threw in at the conclusion of his will, "I give my wife my second-best bed with the furniture." If not insulting, it was ironical and possibly humorous.

The Hathaway timber-frame house preserves a drowsy mien born of hedgerows, lavender, roses and narrow lanes of the English Midlands. The oldest section of the house is of fifteenth-century construction. The cottage was held by the Hathaway descendants until 1892 when it was purchased to be maintained as a memorial, ostensibly for the little-known and forgotten wife — but even here Will Shakespeare seems preeminent.

Some of the Hathaway furnishings have been retained in the cottage — pewter plates, wooden trenchers, powdering tubs for salting meat and a handsomely carved four-poster bed, obviously not Will's "second-best."

An informal garden of aromatic herbs, flowers and fruit trees gives an atmosphere of quaint gentility and grace to Anne Hathaway's thatched-roof cottage.

Time: 9:00 A.M.
Direction: Northwest
Lens: Normal

My timing is rather specific here in that in summer a row of high trees casts dark shadows on this cottage and gardens prior to 9:00 A.M., and just after that hundreds of visitors converge on the cottage. Buses and cars appear from everywhere. Two previous attempts at photographing proved failures, as rain cancelled out hopes of picture taking. This attempt later in August turned out more favorably and the flowers were even more beautiful. Attendants were most helpful in controlling lagging visitors enthralled with a special flower — suggesting politely that other areas offered even more beautiful specimens. This area is typical of the many places one might have to visit several times before catching a little bright sunshine. The English countryside is without equal when the sun shines; yet the green grass and flowering meadow are that way only part of the time. Allow enough time to get a fair share of pictures.

Eilean Donan Castle / Scotland

Eilean Donan Castle — Eilean is a Gaelic word meaning island — is no longer an island-fortress castle because a causeway now joins the island with the mainland, replacing an old ferry. The uniting of tribal kingdoms in the eleventh century A.D. was the beginning of the Scottish Kingdom, and in 1230 A.D Eilean Donan Castle was erected on the site of an ancient fortress. Thus, this castle has been an intimate part of Scottish history. As a fortress in 1331, it held prisoners and the Warden of Scotland ordered the execution of fifty "delinquents." The ghastly and macabre aftermath of this execution was seen when the victims' heads "encircled the castle wall like a chaplet of roses."

Eilean Donan Castle suffered damage from the battering of English warships during the Jacobite insurrection. James III — called "the old Pretender" — and others of the Scottish House of Stuart, instigated the Jacobite (Jacobus = James) uprising to sweep James' German relative George I of the House of Hanover from the English throne, but this movement was unsuccessful.

The western coast of Scotland is a shredded, rocky shore with hundreds of deep inlets and narrow bays stretching inland. These are called *lochs*. It is believed that they were formed by glacial erosion similar to the *viks* of Norway.

The tiny rocky isle on which Eilean Donan Castle is perched is in an inlet called Loch Duich. It is not far from the town of Dornie and the hills called the Five Sisters of Kintail in Inverness-shire in the Scottish Highlands.

The large and powerful Clan Mackenzie has for many centuries claimed Eilean Donan Castle as one of its four or five Clan Seats and ever since Colin, Second Lord Mackenzie, was made Earl of Seaforth, the Seaforth heritage has been attached to the castle.

The name of Clan Macrae is also associated with Eilean Donan for the home of the "Wild Macraes" was also in Kintail. They were related to the Mackenzie Barony of Kintail and served these Earls of Seaforth as constables, chamberlains and vicars. It was the late constable of Eilean Donan Castle, Lt. Colonel John Macrae-Gilstrap, who restored the castle to its present condition. As a small museum and a war memorial it is open to visitors from Easter to mid-September, and if you stop here you will undoubtedly be served tea and scones.

Time: Early morning
Direction: Southwest
Lens: Normal

While we were traveling through Wales one rainy afternoon, a weather forecast indicated a change of weather in northern Scotland. I had for years wanted to photograph Eilean Donan Castle on Loch Duich. A day later, at a little inn near the castle, our host looked to the west and predicted clear weather for the next morning. Up at daybreak, we climbed a nearby hill and, before the winds began, we were fortunate in recording the calm waters of the Loch Duich and its famous little castle. Exposures are normal and the only problem for us was rapidly changing weather, since by noon the sky was overcast again before additional pictures could be made. Yet, the opportunity to photograph this far-off little treasure was to me as rewarding as the Taj Mahal.

Cathedral / Mexico City, Mexico

MEXICO CITY, A THROBBING, VITAL, CAPITAL CITY OF MORE than three million people, lies on a plateau over 7000 feet high where it continues to boom and balloon like an atomic mushroom. In the midst of its skyscrapers, business activities, university life, art exhibits, fiestas and bull fights, the old Cathedral on the Zócalo sits quietly undisturbed, like an old lady quietly rocking and knitting in the midst of a tornado.

Spanish Baroque seems to be a convenient blanket term to cover the various unrelated architectural features that were included during the construction of the Cathedral over a period of one hundred years. Here one can even find contributions of Greek Doric, Ionic and Corinthian capitals.

Even with the great metamorphic growth of Mexico City, the old government buildings surrounding the Zócalo (Constitution Square) have not been destroyed. So it is that the massive gray sandstone Roman Catholic Cathedral still stands at the north end of the open park, the Zócalo.

The cathedral is cruciate in form. Its high, twin bell towers on each side of the elaborate façade have set the pattern for many Spanish churches and cathedrals both in Mexico and in the Southwest of the United States. Originally, the sacred sculptured temple of the Aztec Indians stood on this site in the Indians' watery capital. The Spanish conqueror, Cortez, had the temple destroyed in the early 1500s, and it is claimed that the foundations of the Cathedral on the Zócalo are the broken fragments of the Aztec temple.

The delicate "state of health" of the Cathedral today is due to its basic underpinnings. Mexico City lies in the Valley of Mexico, on the plateau which was once a vast, swampy lake containing many islands on which the Aztecs lived with the insular idea that here they would be safe from enemies. The lake has been drained for centuries but the city still has precarious foundations plus frequent terrifying tremors — earthquakes.

If you can find a bench in the Zócalo where you may relax in the early evening, you may hear all about you the Spanish conversation of the descendants of the early Spaniards and Indians — the mestizos — now internationally known as Mexicans. They still stroll through the gardens as of yore, perhaps with a small recollection or appreciation of their ancestral past, after a busy day at the office.

Time: Dusk
Direction: Northwest
Lens: Normal

For several weeks before and after Christmas, Mexico City is brilliantly lighted for the festive occasion. Though this detailed cathedral is quite black and difficult to portray in color during daylight hours, sundown and many well-placed lights transform the cathedral into a jewel of beauty. Here the lights are turned on by sundown and one exposure with slight variation can record a more pleasing rendering of this famous masterpiece of architecture. A longer exposure increases the effect of car lights. Mexico City probably is unique in the great cities of the world for its elaborate Christmas lighting — with figures often ten stories high on many of its major buildings.

Playa de Cortez / Guaymas, Mexico

BOTH THE PLAYA DE CORTEZ AND THE SEA OF CORTEZ (GULF of California) bear the name of the bold Spaniard who was doubtless the greatest Spanish conqueror of the New World, Cortez or Cortés. History of Mexico is termited with his name and exploits and his ruthless cruelty to the natives.

He established the first settlement in Baja California (Lower California) when exploring this area; thus the name of Hernando Cortez still floats over the green-blue gulf and rests on its *playas* — shore and beaches.

The hotel called Playa de Cortez at Guaymas, Sonora, Mexico, does not belong to the age of the early Spanish explorer, but one feels as he steps through the handsome gateway that he is entering a colorful old hacienda swathed in brilliant bougainvillea. Architecturally it is true hacienda style, and its furnishings are in delightful keeping with its exterior.

Bacochibampo Bay fans out in front of the hotel sheltering other resorts which line its shore, the *playa*. This glittering bay with a few off-shore islands attracts fishermen, sun-lovers and watersprites. At day's end jocular record-fish stories are routinely exchanged between the deep-sea fishermen. In this subtropical spa, water skiers, sailors, swimmers, snorkelers and relaxed beach-tanners all have tales to swap at the sunset hour.

There is a real plus for visitors in the lethargic old town of San José de Guaymas only a few miles southeast of la Playa de Cortez. With its superb land-locked harbor it is surprising that Guaymas has not become a greater seaport. The majority of ships which dock in the harbor are small boats of the shrimp fleet. Guaymas shrimp — large prawns — have gained national distinction and shrimp fishing has become the main industry of the town.

The buildings, of course, have been somewhat updated throughout the years, but the town seems to have fallen less into the pattern of modernity than many Mexican towns. The old Cathedral stands as is customary — on the town square — and homes, in old Spanish tradition, have their front walls facing flatly to the street with their intimate living quarters and gardens lying behind closed doors. From the hills behind Guaymas there is an expansive view of the beautiful bay with the Gulf of California in the distance.

Father Kino, the Jesuit priest whose unflagging zeal established missions throughout the Mexican state of Sonora and even on north into Arizona, left us the first historical account of San José de Guaymas, beginning in 1680.

Presently the unhurried town of Guaymas gives no hint of the original inhabitants, the Guaymenos Indians, nor of the stormy days of French adventurers or pirates seeking gold. Only the aftermath of the Spanish conquest of Mexico is evident here today.

Time: Sunset
Direction: West
Lens: Normal

Sunsets have been my most interesting challenge in photography. My first major sale was of one photograph made in 1939, and I think that to date I have attempted more than any other photographer. Though I have been able to sell hundreds of such pictures, my greatest thrill is this inspiring phenomenon itself. An occasional spectacular display is as exhilarating as any sight I've ever seen. In the desert of Arizona, water is a scarcity and it is obvious that a body of water nearly doubles the effect of the sunset. At the beautiful bay of the Playa de Cortez, with its volcanic peaks on the horizon, I have tried for a dozen years to capture such a sunset. Only once was I successful. Exposure for such a sight is quite simple. An actual meter reading of the brightest area of light is a starting point with slight variations for density changes. Use a tripod and sufficient film.

Machu Picchu / Peru, South America

A HUMAN FLYING OVER THE ANDES MOUNTAINS AT AN ALTItude of 20,000 feet and looking down on Machu Picchu could imagine it to be a roofless, moldy beehive — an empty honeycomb dropped on a Peruvian peak and forgotten.

For what purpose did the Incas — Quechua Indians — use this bizarre isolated town? It lay nearly 5000 feet below their thriving capital of Cuzco which is a breathless 11,000 feet above sea level. Machu Picchu is fifty miles from Cuzco.

Built on a sheer, rocky peak where two sides drop a vertical 2000 feet into the valley, there was very little space for any agricultural pursuits on rocky, tiered, terraced hillsides. On the third side of Machu Picchu (Old Peak) the Young Peak (Huayna Picchu) rises, not yet shrunk with age.

Several possibilities for the existence of Machu Picchu have been popularized. The obvious one seems to be that it was a specially fortified town to be used in extremity. A second, more fanciful idea assumes that it may have been used for a harem since female skeletons predominate in the excavations. It was destroyed in the mid-1500s by the Spanish Conquistador Pizarro in his conquest of the Inca Empire. It was rediscovered four centuries later in 1911 — shrouded in vegetation similar to Angkor — by Professor Hiram Bingham of Yale University.

Roofless rooms, courtyards, storehouses, a stairway and temple are built upward following the contour of the peak. Caste, in a sense, was recognized. Nobility had precedence and lived at the highest and most impregnable point near the temple. Military and peasants lived on descending levels. Sun worshipers, the Incas placed the Sun Temple at the apex of this pyramidal town. Tradition says that the Sun Priest in his feathered robes assured his people by his ministrations at the high altar that he had stopped the sun as it seemed to hesitate on its northward journey — the winter solstice — and that they would not be left in darkness. The sun would return to them on its accustomed course. And it always did!

Following Professor Bingham's exciting discovery in 1911, several expeditions of archaeologists have lifted the veil from this last Inca stronghold, destroyed by man and slowly disintegrated by nature.

Today it is possible to reach these ruins of Machu Picchu from the town of Cuzco by rail and bus. From Cuzco, a downgrade trip so exhilarating that you either sit like a body in deepfreeze or embrace it with full and fatalistic enjoyment is a sensational journey. By bus you ascend from the Urubamba River two thousand feet via switchbacks over five miles of Hiram Bingham Highway in relative comfort — especially as compared to straddling a burro over a trail, the only means of access before 1948.

Time: Midmorning
Direction: Northeast
Lens: Normal

Storms occurred each day but fortunately the sky remained clear until about ten o'clock both mornings. Deep greens reflect less than normal light. Direct meter reading of dark rock or typical green area is suggested. Though I often hire models for commercial pictures, I have used none in this book that would not be available to any traveler. A little extra color is often a help. No mention of hotels and other services has been included in the text, yet this area is 115 kilometers by electric car-train from Cuzco and I highly recommend that one stay overnight at the small hotel at the ruins — the area should be seen both in the evening and morning. Don't let bad weather disappoint you in your photographic possibilities. Lifting clouds in these 12,000-foot Andes peaks can be most rewarding.

Mt. Osorno / Southern Chile

FOR CENTURIES THE ENGLISH LAKE COUNTRY HAS BEEN AN objective of European travelers. Now, at the other end of the globe, the Chilean lake country is attracting many visitors because of its remarkable beauty.

When one speaks casually of the "Chilean lake country" it usually includes the lakes in Argentina which are a part of this chain of blue gems, since these lakes almost meet at the border of these two countries.

A small boat transports travelers westward from the town of San Carlos de Bariloche in the Argentine, through a series of azure lakes in which the majestic Andes are reflected. By bus or car the border is crossed through a low, forested pass in the Andes and you are in the Chilean lake country.

The climax of this trip is the awesome and breathtaking view of snow-covered Mt. Osorno rising before you in perfect symmetry and beauty, 8730 feet above sea level. Often, like Narcissus, it can admire its own reflection in the Lago Todos los Santos. This Lake of All Saints is a kaleidascope of blues, the color varying with time, weather and temperature. The calm beauty of Mt. Osorno was disturbed in 1960 when this volcano last erupted.

German colonists who migrated to southern Chile in mid-century have done much for Chile's culture. From their homes on the shores of this lake they still come out to the passing tourist boat to pick up their mail and supplies.

Time: Morning
Direction: North
Lens: Normal

This beautiful symmetrical peak lay covered with a new mantle of snow after two weeks of cloudy weather that hid it from view. The lake trip offers many views from the cruise boat, but another possibility from shore again offers a little extra foreground color. Normal exposure is recommended, though a faster shutter speed is suggested if photographing from the boat deck.

Rio Harbor / Rio de Janeiro, Brazil

THE MONTH OF JANUARY WAS CORRECT, JANEIRO. THE RIVER, Rio, was a figment of the imagination of the Portuguese navigator who entered this harbor on New Year's Day in 1502. It was reasonable that such a commodious harbor should be the mouth of a great river, but it wasn't the fact.

Throughout the world the "most beautiful, largest, oldest," always cause competitive language. But Rio Harbor's topography and simple beauty put it in a commanding position among harbors. Sugar Loaf means but one thing worldwide, the granite stud 1300 feet high rising out of the waters of Guanabara Bay like a bulbous stone arrowhead. The full panoramic view of the city, its beaches, buildings and suburbs from Sugar Loaf is worth the swaying cable-car ride one takes to reach this peak.

On Corcovado (Hunchback) Mountain is the Brazilian Christ of the Redeemer, a 130-foot concrete statue of Christ with outstretched arms 1200 feet above the sea.

Conversely, in the Cordilleras stretching the length of the western coast of South America the great metal statue of the Christ of the Andes 12,000 feet above the sea, symbolizes perpetual peace between Chile and Argentina. Few ever see the Andes Christ because of its inaccessibility and the fog or clouds which surround it much of the time.

Almost unknown to North Americans, the third monumental Cristo Rey marks the junction of Texas, Mexico and New Mexico where this giant stone sculpturing looks down the Rio Grande along the borderline between the United States and Mexico.

Brazil — meaning a red dyewood early exported from here — occupies almost one half of the South American continent. Since the departure of its Portuguese kings and rulers by means of a revolution in 1889, it has become a Republic with a five-year term for the President.

By 1888 all of the African slaves who had been transported here to work on the big fazendas were liberated. The plaintive Fado music one hears sung in Portugal today is said to have originated with the homesick Negroes who were slaves in Brazil.

It is well to prompt the weatherman ahead of a visit to Rio Harbor to furnish good weather — and clear atmosphere. Often this magnificent view is a bitter disappointment for haze and fog, our modern smog — this creeping evil of the world — can completely obscure the harbor view.

Time: Slightly past sundown
Direction: East
Lens: Normal

City smoke and smog are not limited to a few better known American cities. European cities and the great industrial cities of South America have their problems too. To minimize this effect, evening light was chosen with a balanced lighting between the sky's glow and the city lights. The vantage point was high up the road toward the Corcovado statue of Christ.

Trunk Bay / St. John Island, Virgin Islands

TRUNK BAY, A CARIB-BLUE, SHELL-SHAPED COVE FLUTED with sparkling white sand, does not take its name from any pirate's treasure trunk buried here, but from the Trunk Turtle which was once abundant in these off-shore waters. When the Indian mongoose was injected into St. John to destroy snakes and rats, as usual its unlimited diet included ground birds and freshly laid turtle eggs. Thus the Trunk Turtle has been decimated.

About one hundred Virgin Islands lying east of Puerto Rico belong in the group known as The Lesser Antilles of the Caribbean. The British Virgins are farthest east and the Virgin Islands of the United States lie nearest to Puerto Rico. The three largest American Virgins, St. Croix, St. Thomas and St. John, were known for two hundred years as the Danish West Indies. Then, during World War I, Denmark sold them to the United States as a measure of protection for the Panama Canal Zone.

St. John — twenty square miles — is the smallest of the triad and is still delightfully non-touristic. Mr. Laurance S. Rockefeller, with keen appreciation of the rare beauty of St. John, gave property covering more than three-fourths of the island to be used in the creation of a national park. The dedication of this twenty-ninth national park of the United States occurred in 1956.

The jurisdiction of the National Park Service extends one-half mile off-shore where coral gardens and brilliant under-sea life are visible. The Park Service protects both land and sea areas from vandalism, spear fishing and commercial fishing for the pure enjoyment of visitors.

St. John harbors a string of pure-white sand beaches as yet untarnished by man's defections. The island is a luxurious natural laboratory for botanists with giant ferns, orchids and a myriad of botanical delicacies.

Danish sugarcane plantations on St. John were operated with African slave labor. There are still evidences of some of the masters' "great houses," sugar mills and windmill towers. The Park Service has done much to stabilize the windmill on the Caneel Bay Plantation.

Romancers do not differentiate between pirates, privateers and buccaneers. In the Caribbean the *boucan* (French) was a frame for smoking raw meat in order to preserve it. The *Boucaniers* (Buccaneers), a heterogeneous group of rovers who unlawfully helped themselves to cattle where they found them, butchered them and smoked their beef on *boucans*. It is said that the plantation owners and the natives hired these capable butchers to slaughter their private stock of cattle, pigs and goats and to cure the meat for them.

Trunk Bay is just a virginal corner of St. John Island where one occasionally sees a swimmer or a boat which brings into focus that this perfect beach is a reality.

Time: Morning
Direction: North
Lens: Normal

Usually a framing will add a third dimension to a scenic vista. Because this is a national park one must be careful not to destroy vegetation for a better camera position. Often a cooperative park ranger or naturalist will assist with branch removal if he is asked and if your request is reasonable. It often offers him the opportunity to show others a good picture location. Here I experienced my first hurricane. The beach was littered with coconuts and the blue water turned brown with mud. Five days later it cleared and it looked as if it had always been a peaceful coral beach.

Moraine Lake / Banff National Park, Canada

THE CANADIAN ROCKY MOUNTAINS ARE SO SATURATED WITH sapphire, emerald and turquoise lakes that Moraine Lake which is only about forty miles from the famous Lake Louise in Banff National Park has been less publicized in travel folders than even more inaccessible lakes. Its rare setting in the Valley of the Ten Peaks makes the calm blue surface of Moraine Lake a multiple mirror.

We were the only trespassers on the lake one morning, drifting, silently awed by the majesty of our surroundings. A monarch butterfly joined us, alighting on the thwart of our rowboat where he leisurely fanned himself with his brilliant orange and black wings.

Along the rocky edge of the lake a Dipper or water ouzel, a chunky wren-like bird, was bobbing up and down like a hiccup.

With his mind on his business he would run completely beneath the surface of the lake, poke under rocks hunting for aquatic insects or small fish for his fledglings. Then with only a slight swish of his tail he was off to a nearby nest on the wet mossy ledge of an overhanging rock.

Time: Midmorning
Direction: South
Lens: Moderate and wide angle

Often the lake is frozen as late as June or early July. Rainfall can be heavy through June, yet it is at this early summer period when the mountains are still beautifully snow covered. Exposure is rather hard to judge due to brightness of snow and sky, yet darker tree and water areas must be the basis for an accurate reading. Again, I suggest bracketing the meter reading. Take the professional's attitude that you are not trying to prove how you can do it in one exposure. Film is your least expensive commodity in photography of subjects around the world.

Covered Bridge / Bath, New Hampshire

TWO HUNDRED BIRTHDAY CANDLES WERE REQUIRED TO ILLUminate the Bicentennial celebrations of Bath, New Hampshire, in 1965. Two hundred years ago, in 1765, Bath became a community. One citizen of Bath frankly declares, "The Indians were here first and it therefore seems piddling to quarrel about priorities."

There are three covered bridges in Bath but this one in the village is an especially choice composition for photographers, with the church spire as an eye-reaching background. This old wooden bridge with many original timbers still linked by wooden pegs, crosses both the Ammonoosuc River and the railroad tracks with its 400-foot span. Built in 1832, it was a boastful 133 years old at the time of the Bicentennial festivities.

An autobiography of a covered bridge would provide imaginative and realistic material for those of us who are sentimentalists. The clop of shod hoofs, the plodding of oxen, the creak of wagons and carts, the rumbling of carriages, the slithering of sleigh runners and even the sound of soft voices of young lovers rendezvousing under the dim kerosene lights of the bridge could be made characters in the self-history of the bridge. On a stormy Sunday, a hypothetical Ebenezer would hitch his horse and surrey on the bridge while the family attended church.

A severe penalty of one dollar ($1.00) was exacted for driving a team over the bridge faster than a walk. A sign so indicated and the law was strictly enforced. A skittish horse frightened by the noisy Ammonoosuc swirling under him was no excuse. A driver could always descend and, holding the bridle, lead his horse across the bridge *at a walk*.

The history of this delightful New England town is full of the everyday business of birth, life and death. Historical anecdotes written by its citizens in the *Historical Notes of Bath, New Hampshire, 1765–1965*, published for its Bicentennial, are illuminating and thoroughly enjoyable.

Bath as a democratic community believes in equality, but also, as a discriminating community, that "some are more equal than others," but when we use the term First Families we have primarily in mind those families which came here first and have been here the longest. . . .

Preachers could not stand the wear and tear imposed on them. An advertisement reads: "Wanted: A preacher to suit a few people in Bath . . . only the application of an Angel with an angelic wife and daughter will be considered. The wife can be a Sabbath School teacher; the daughter can have frequent 'rides' after a span. The pastor must never exhibit a desire for anything."

One broad-minded citizen who married the widow Chamberlain had the epitaph on his tombstone neatly inscribed to himself, the former husband Chamberlain, and to "Their Widow" Sarah.

Bath, New Hampshire, was named after Bath, England, but lays no claim to being a mineral water spa nor of entertaining musical salons. However, at a very early date, one of its citizens had a pipe organ in his home "reaching from floor to ceiling."

New England and the eastern seaboard of the United States have no exclusive claim to covered bridges, only priority of date. One thousand covered bridges have been built west of the Rocky Mountains since pioneers first trekked west in covered wagons. The state of Washington has more covered bridges than any other state of the Union.

Many writers have immortalized covered bridges. We are grateful to Bath, its citizens and its librarian for the background story of its bridge, possibly the most famous covered bridge in the United States.

Time: Morning
Direction: Northeast
Lens: Normal

Though exposure is quite simple, timing for photography of fall color is important. Normal dates for the first color often vary. Dryness of the season and late or early color cannot be forecast too well. A call to a friendly ranger at the National Forest Service office nearby will give you your best advice. These managers of our forest wealth are also doing their part in the job of assisting with recreation for our nature lovers. Bath, with its long, covered bridge, is a typical New England scene. A little scouting for a vantage point can result in a new picture of an old theme.

Old Faithful/Yellowstone National Park, Wyoming

EVEN BITTER WYOMING WINTERS DOWN TO 40 TO 50 DEGREES below zero Fahrenheit do not stop Old Faithful from her performance. "The show must go on" for this prima donna whether the spectators are animals hovering near this sky-climbing spiggot for warmth or humans in the heat of summer standing agape and squinting through their viewfinders in the presence of this mighty miracle.

In Yellowstone National Park the hot springs, pools and geysers are not controlled by a man-made thermostat. After the earthquake of 1959 here it was found that the average thermal heat had been lowered by ten degrees and that new geysers had erupted.

No one would believe John Colter in 1810 when he told of having seen this natural phenomenon at the time when he was running from the Indians. Doubtless a hallucination! Among the thermal spots in the world, those of New Zealand, Iceland and Yellowstone are the most extensive, with Yellowstone topping the list. Iceland has given us its word *geysir* — our geyser, which means gusher or rager.

Old Faithful, named by General Washburn on his 1870 expedition, erupts at intervals of from 33 to 95 minutes, making the average interval one hour. Climbing in spasms higher and higher like a bouncing ball, it attains 115 to 180 feet altitude and sends its column of steam to 1000 feet in the air.

Old Faithful's greatest competitor in the park is the Grand Geyser which shoots its water and steam 200 feet upward, but this geyser keeps its audience waiting over a period of 18 to 19 hours between shows.

Yellowstone was established as our first National Park by Congress in 1872. Indeed, it was the world's first national park. Today it draws visitors from every state in the Union and some from foreign countries.

Thousands of colorful license plates on cars parked side by side near Old Faithful give the effect of a babel of geography. This rare National Park has more facets and variety, even aside from the thermal area, than any other United States National Park.

Time: Afternoon
Direction: North
Lens: Normal

Perhaps the most important consideration is the direction of the wind when photographing this particular geyser. A slightly underexposed sky is advisable due to the great expanses of brilliant white when the sun strikes the water vapor. It is also important that your choice of camera position is one that will not be in a crowded area where numerous people will come and stand between you and the geyser.

Monument Valley / Arizona—Utah

RAY MANLEY HAS MADE MORE THAN FIFTY TRIPS TO MONU-ment Valley to photograph this matchless Navajo country under all possible conditions. He has chosen this picture to portray its mood of beauty, majesty and simplicity. Monument Valley lies largely in the northeast corner of Arizona and is part of the "Four Corners Country." A renowned American geologist has described its formation in clear layman's language for us. He says:

No other area on the earth presents such grandeur and variety in such simple geological terms as does the Colorado Plateau in northern Arizona and adjacent parts of Utah, Colorado and New Mexico which make the only "four corners" in the United States. The rocks are essentially horizontal beds of sandstones, shales and limestones which have been slowly uplifted through eons of time. The Colorado River had established itself before the uplift began and has been able to cut its bed downward quite as fast as the rate of uplift. Thus the Grand Canyon is but another river valley, but it is the most spectacular one on earth because of the beauty and structure of the rocks through which it has cut its bed and because it exposes the greatest cross section of history of any valley or canyon on earth. More than two billion years difference in age is revealed between the rocks in the bottom of the canyon and those at the top.

Geologically speaking, perhaps the simplest of the many dramatic features of the Colorado Plateau country is Monument Valley. Except for such features as the ragged peak of Agathla the monuments from the tall thin spires to the larger buttes and broader mesas are but remnants of massive beds of sandstone and minor amounts of shale which constitute a continuous surface or level represented by the tops of the buttes and mesas. Differential erosion tells the story.

The Navajos, originally farmers living near the Pueblo Indians, became more nomadic and belligerent after the Spaniards and Americans invaded the Southwest. Partly in retaliation, they raided, stole sheep, goats, and horses, and plundered the country-side aided by their new transportation — horses — which the Spaniards had introduced. Finally seized from their canyon hide-outs by American troops and taken to Fort Sumner in New Mexico, the Navajos saw the handwriting on the wall and agreed to peace. They were moved by the U.S. Government to their present Navajo Reservation — sixteen million acres in Arizona, Utah and New Mexico where more than 100,000 Navajos live today. Today they are good citizens of the United States. You can still see many of them, whose lineal descent is through the mother, living in their native *hogans* and clinging to their Navajo customs and traditions. They are still silversmiths (a craft they began after their return from Fort Sumner), rug weavers and sheepherders, and many of the women wear the colorful Navajo velvet jackets and full squaw skirts. But many are also modern Navajos.

Harry Goulding, the white man who came here in the early 1920s to buy sheep, is the father, brother and cousin of the Navajos in Monument Valley, knowing all of their joys and tribulations, customs and thinking, and speaking their language fluently. Living first in tents, Harry and his fine wife, Mike, later built a trading station and now have a comfortable guest lodge set against the red cliffs, almost invisible to tourists driving through the valley. When the Depression hit in the early 1930s, Harry, with hat in hand, persuaded Hollywood producers to make use of this magnificent setting, an arrangement which lessened the financial distress of the Indians then. He also gave land for the present Indian hospital here.

Today this Navajo Reservation, so long "good for nothing," is boiling up with hidden wealth — oil, gas, uranium — and the "poor Indians" are fast becoming "rich Navajos."

Time: Late afternoon — summer
Direction: East
Lens: Normal

Though poor photographic weather is very unusual here, an occasional storm can offer challenging light. Good photographic possibilities remain until after sunset. Use direct meter reading with bracketing or additional exposures.

Havasu Falls / Grand Canyon, Arizona

THERE IS MATCHLESS BEAUTY AND INTIMACY IN THE BLUE-green waterfalls of Havasu Canyon. There is august beauty in huge majestic falls such as Victoria, Africa, and Iguassu, Brazil, but for pure enchantment Havasu Falls transcends them.

Havasu Creek, originating in springs, flows through the pocket-sized Indian reservation of the Havasupai (green-blue-water people) to irrigate their farms, peach orchards and gardens. On its exit from the vale surrounded by sheer red canyon walls, Havasu Creek forges four exquisite waterfalls on its way to join the Colorado River of the Grand Canyon.

Havasu Canyon has been the home of a small tribe of Southwest Indians — about 300 of them now — for more than one thousand years, but no man knows how many milleniums this blue-green stream has been chiseling its course through rocky walls bordering the Colorado River.

You may sit in quiet repose before Havasu Falls and absorb its shining and pulsing rhythm. With an azure blue sky above it, the green-blue water of the falls emerges through a travertine channel and drops into shallow basins or pools, 110 feet below, overflows their brims and moves on to the river. The receding tiers of travertine pools look like overlapping seashells stacked casually together.

Contiguous to the falls and hanging from the top of the cliff are buff-colored curtains of travertine, draped by the master exterior decorator. In areas where limestone prevails, spring waters are impregnated with the calcium from the limestone. Havasu Falls in its descent through the centuries has deposited calcium from its spray on the surrounding areas, thus forming both the porous curtains of travertine or sinter, and the numerous shallow basins beneath it.

If you yearn to see Havasu Falls — and who does not — you can reach it on foot or by horses provided by the Havasu Indians. Horses are brought to Hilltop which is 35 miles west of El Tovar Hotel at Grand Canyon. Topocoba trail descends from Hilltop with switchbacks for 1000 feet and levels off into a valley canyon which leads to the Havasupai Reservation. With sufficient rib-kicking and urging you will make the trail mileage on the poky Indian horse in about three hours. On shanks' mare, your own footwork will determine the time on the trail, probably most of the day. Take your own food. Water is plentiful. Camping grounds are several miles beyond the Reservation. There are a few tenderfoot accommodations with plumbing and a communal stove in the Supai village but you must make reservations well in advance to secure them.

On our first trip into Havasu Canyon, my husband, photographing as he went, descended into the canyon by helicopter, the first chopper to alight in the canyon. Steel beams were being "copted" into Supai piecemeal to construct a new church for the Protestant mission established there many years ago. His "house-wife" followed slowly by trail on an Indian horse accompanied by two press photographers who were not in training for their first experience astride and who were vociferous about it being their first and last horseback ride. But from the gracious and kindly missionary who rode the trail with us, we learned many intimate things of this isolated tribe of our first Americans.

Time: Early afternoon — early summer
Direction: East
Lens: Wide angle

Timing is very important if full sunlight is desired. The falls face in a westerly direction and are in a very deep canyon. The sunlight illuminates the falls from about 1:00 P.M. until 3:30 when high canyon walls cast their shadows across the area. The time of year selected should be as near to June 21 — the longest day — as possible, but at least between May and mid-August. However, late July and August could bring summer storms and dangerous flash-flooding, discoloring the water. Exposure can be varied for the water motion effect desired.

Arizona Sunset

THIS FAMOUS PHOTOGRAPH OF RAY MANLEY'S HAS BEEN SEEN around the world. The Arizona desert at sunset with the saguaro cactus and the cowboy and his horse could be Arizona's crest.

We have girdled the earth and have been from the Arctic into the Antarctic but nowhere — yea not anywhere — have we seen sunsets comparable to those of Arizona, our forty-eighth state. It is a fact that there are more hours of sunshine and more clear days in Arizona than in any other state of the Union. After much research, the largest solar telescope in the world was located in the Arizona desert where astronomers must make reservations in advance to take their turn viewing the sun.

The sun-bronzed Spaniards who came north from Mexico in 1540 seeking gold in the chimerical Seven Cities of Cibola were crestfallen to find that their goal, the Zuni pueblos, were gilded only by the rays of the setting sun. Later explorers, however, did find deposits of the precious gold — as well as silver — in what is today southern Arizona and northern Sonora, Mexico. To clarify which area was being referred to, the Spaniards designated the Southern Arizona region as the "District of Arizonac," the name being taken from a mission station with rich silver deposits nearby. The word "Arizonac" is believed to be derived from the Papago Indian words *ali* (small) and *shonak* (place of the spring) — thus "place of the small spring."

A sunset! There is no such thing, for the sun neither sits nor sets. This "apparent daily descent of the sun below the horizon" must revert to the ancient days when the earth was believed to be flat. Ol' Sol hangs in his own sphere in the heavens. As we rotate we anticipate his crepuscular evensong — a sunset.

Unbelievable sunsets are so identified with Arizona that even the Arizona flag displays a sunset, with red and golden rays of the sun over a lower field of midnight blue. In Arizona the sunset is a flaming curtain slowly drawn back to expose a dark stage where the Moon is the prima donna and the actors are all Stars.

Time: Sundown
Direction: West
Lens: Normal — long

Though sunsets occur throughout the world, the western United States and the great desert area of Arizona in particular are without rival in their displays of the most colorful and frequent spectacles. Exposure is made by direct reading of brightest area and bracketing for brighter or deeper effects.